Tina Thoburn

Virginia Arnold

Rita Schlatterbeck

Ann Terry

Macmillan English

SERIES E ®

Macmillan Publishing Co., Inc.
New York

Collier Macmillan Publishers
London

ACKNOWLEDGMENTS

The publisher gratefully acknowledges permission to reprint the following copyrighted material:

"Secret Places" from *Secret Places* by D. J. Arneson. Copyright © 1971 by Don Jon Arneson.

"Bus Ride" from "Ferry Ride" from *City Child* by Selma Robinson. Copyright 1931, © 1959 by Selma Robinson. Reprinted by permission of Holt, Rinehart and Winston, Publishers.

"Song of the Train" from *Far and Few* by David McCord. Copyright 1952 by David McCord. Reprinted by permission of Little, Brown and Company in association with the Atlantic Monthly Press.

"Tom Sawyer — Fence Washer" by Steven Otfinoski. Copyright © 1982 by Macmillan Publishing Co., Inc.

"I Can Be . . ." from the book *I Can Be . . .* by A. K. Roche. Copyright © 1967 by A. K. Roche. Published by Prentice-Hall, Inc., Englewood Cliffs, New Jersey.

"Blaze Finds the Trail" by C. W. Anderson. Reprinted with permission of Macmillan Publishing Co., Inc. from *Blaze Finds the Trail*. Copyright © 1950 by Macmillan Publishing Co., Inc., renewed 1978 by Phyllis Anderson Wood.

"Chinese Brush Painting" from *The Zoom Catalog* by WGBH Educational Foundation. Copyright © 1972 by WGBH Educational Foundation. Reprinted by permission of Random House, Inc.

"The Surprise Party" reprinted with permission of Macmillan Publishing Co., Inc. from *The Surprise Party* by Pat Hutchins. *The Surprise Party* by Pat Hutchins is published in the United Kingdom by The Bodley Head.

Cover design: Nadja Furlan

Illustration Credits:
Gwen Connell, Mac Conner, Len Ebert, Fred Harsh, Marilyn Janovitz, Verlin Miller, Hima Pamoedjo, Jan Pyk, Helen Rodewig, Mario Stasolla, Robert Steele, Walter Velez

Photography Credits:
Clara Aich, Peter Arnold Photo Archives, Harvey Lloyd; P.F. Collier, Inc.; Colour Library International (USA) Ltd.; Leo DeWys, Inc., Everett C. Johnson; Lawrence Frank; Pam Hasacawa; International Stock Photo; Monkmeyer Press Photo, Mimi Forsyth; Sigrid Owen; *Photo Researchers, Inc.,* ©Ron Church, ©W.V. Crich, ©Allan D. Cruikshank, ©Rudolff Freund, ©Lowell Georgia, ©Fran Hall, ©R.C. Hermes/National Audubon Society Division, ©Russ Kinne, ©Susan McCartney, ©Yoichi R. Okamoto, ©Paul E. Taylor/National Audobon Society Division; Shostal Associates, Richard F. Zind; Tom Stack and Associates; *The Stock Market,* ©Ed Goldfarb, ©Robin Lehman, ©Roy Morsch

Parts of this work were published in earlier editions of SERIES E: Macmillan English.

Macmillan Publishing Co., Inc.
866 Third Avenue, New York, New York 10022
Collier Macmillan Canada, Inc.

Printed in the United States of America

9 8 7 6 5 4

TABLE OF CONTENTS

Unit 1

Unit 2

Unit 3

Unit 4

Unit 5

Unit 6

Unit 7

Unit 8

PACIFIC MARINELAND

Grammar and Related Language Skills

Sentences
Three Kinds of Sentences
Punctuation for Sentences
Parts of Telling Sentences
Building Sentences

Practical Communication

STUDY AND REFERENCE SKILLS
Using the Parts of a Book

COMPOSITION
Writing a Time-Order Paragraph

Creative Expression

A Story

Have you ever seen a porpoise perform? People who teach animals are called animal trainers. Trainers work long and hard to communicate well with the animals. Sometimes trainers want to write about their training experiences. What writing skills would they need? What speaking skills would help trainers communicate well with the animals?

Learning About Sentences

You use words every day. You put words together to explain your ideas to other people. Some groups of words do not make sense. They do not tell enough to show a complete idea. Other groups of words make sense. They state a complete idea.

A **sentence** is a group of words that states a complete idea.

• Read these two groups of words.

The tiger hides behind a tree.   The tiger.

The first group of words states a complete idea. It tells about a tiger, and it tells what the tiger does. The first group of words is a sentence. The second group of words names a tiger, but it does not tell what the tiger does. The second group of words is not a sentence.

The words in a sentence must also come in an order that people can understand. The words state a complete idea when they are in the right order.

• Read these two groups of words.

Three deer nibbled grass. Nibbled three grass deer.

The first group of words states a complete idea. The words are in the right order to make a sentence. The second group of words is not in the right order to make a sentence.

Talk About It

Read the groups of words in each pair. Which group of words is a sentence?

1. Many animals.
Many animals live at the zoo.

2. Two lions.
Two lions eat meat.

Read the groups of words in each pair. Which group of words is in the right order?

3. Swam in the lake a frog.
A frog swam in the lake.

4. The puppy chased a ball.
Chased a ball the puppy.

Skills Practice

Read the groups of words in each pair. Write each group of words that is a sentence.

1. A turtle.
A turtle crawled to a fence.

3. A deer drank water.
A deer.

2. Some birds flew to the nest.
Some birds.

4. The seal.
The seal ate fish.

Read each group of words. Write the group of words that is in the right order to make a sentence.

5. Climbs a the tree monkey.
The monkey climbs a tree.

7. A child fed the lamb.
The fed a lamb child.

6. A bear swam in the pond.
The in pond swam bear a.

8. To zoo the is fun trip a.
A trip to the zoo is fun.

Sample Answers **1.** A turtle crawled to a fence.
5. The monkey climbs a tree.

Three Kinds of Sentences

You use different kinds of sentences every day. Sometimes you use sentences to *tell* something. Sometimes you use sentences to *ask* something. Sometimes you use sentences to *show strong feeling*.

A **telling sentence** is a sentence that tells something.

A **question sentence** is a sentence that asks something.

An **exclamation sentence** is a sentence that shows strong feeling.

- Read each sentence about the picture. Is it a telling sentence, a question sentence, or an exclamation sentence?

The hen eats corn.   Two children feed the raccoon.
Do you see a door?   How nicely the cat plays!

- Look at the picture. Make up one telling sentence about the monkey. Make up one question sentence about the rabbits. Make up one exclamation sentence about the chicken.

Talk About It

Read each sentence. Is it a telling sentence, a question sentence, or an exclamation sentence? Give a reason for each answer.

1. Do you have a pet?
2. I have a monkey and a cat.
3. Is it hard to take care of a monkey?
4. The monkey gets into trouble.
5. What a bad monkey it is!

Skills Practice

Read each sentence. Write **telling** if it is a telling sentence. Write **question** if it is a question sentence. Write **exclamation** if it is an exclamation sentence.

1. We saw an elephant at the zoo.
2. Was the elephant very big?
3. What a huge elephant it was!
4. It splashed water on us.
5. Next we saw some bears.
6. How hungry the bears looked!
7. Did you see any monkeys?
8. We saw many monkeys.
9. Have you ever been to a zoo?

Sample Answer   1. Telling

Capitalizing and Punctuating Sentences

When you talk, your voice gives signs that help people understand you. You take a short rest at the end of each sentence. Your voice is often higher at the end of a question. Your voice can express strong feeling.

● Listen while your teacher reads this story. Listen to hear when each sentence begins and when it ends. Try to hear which sentences are question sentences. Which sentence expresses strong feeling?

How cold the dragon felt! Winter was coming. It had no warm place to stay. What could it do?

The dragon hunted and hunted. At last it found a dry cave.

The dragon was still cold. How do you think it warmed up the cave?

When you write sentences, you need to show where each sentence begins and where it ends.

Use a **capital letter** to begin the first word of every sentence.

S ome snakes sleep all winter.
D o cows sleep all winter?
H ow funny my cat looks!

● Look at the story again. How do the sentences begin?

Use a **period** (.) at the end of a telling sentence.

Many horses sleep standing up .

Use a **question mark** (**?**) at the end
of a question sentence.
How do other animals sleep?

Use an **exclamation mark** (**!**) at
the end of an exclamation sentence.
What a sleepy dog that is!

● Look at the story again. How do the sentences end?

Talk About It

Look at the beginning and end of each sentence.
What special signs are missing in each sentence?

1. i have a pet duck.   **3.** how funny it is!
2. Can you see it   **4.** i will feed it now

Skills Practice

Some special signs are missing in each sentence.
Write each sentence correctly.

1. my dog was lost.   **4.** What was he doing
2. where did you find him?   **5.** he was sleeping
3. He was under a bush   **6.** how happy he was!

Writing Sentences

Pretend that the zoo has a new kind of animal.
It is part raccoon and part duck.

1. Write a question sentence about the animal.
2. Write a telling sentence about the animal.
3. Write an exclamation sentence about the animal.

Sample Answer **1.** My dog was lost.

Skills Review

Read the groups of words in each pair. One group
in each pair is a sentence. It states a complete idea.
Write the sentence in each pair.

1. The children fed the ducks.
   The children.

2. The monkey.
   The monkey ate bananas.

3. An owl.
   An owl fell asleep.

4. A goat walked past.
   A goat.

5. Some lions.
   Some lions roared.

6. The frog hopped away.
   The frog.

Read the groups of words in each pair. Write the
group of words that is in the right order to make a
sentence.

7. A dog into the ran yard.
   A dog ran into the yard.

8. A dog followed Ben home.
   Ben a dog followed home.

9. To the dog Ben called.
   Ben called to the dog.

10. Ben and the dog played.
    And the Ben dog played.

11. Fed the dog Ben.
    Ben fed the dog.

12. Ate the dog.
    The dog ate.

13. The dog came to Ben.
    The dog Ben to came.

14. Dog asleep fell the.
    The dog fell asleep.

Look at each sentence. Write **telling** if it is a telling sentence. Write **question** if it is a question sentence. Write **exclamation** if it is an exclamation sentence.

15. Mae and Nancy went to the pet store.
16. How big the store is!
17. Have you ever been to a pet store?
18. Did you want to buy a pet?
19. The children wanted to buy the kittens.
20. What a sweet kitten that is!

Look at the beginning and end of each sentence.
Some special signs are missing in each sentence.
Write each sentence correctly.

21. the bear has warm fur.
22. What color is the fur
23. It is brown

24. did you hear that noise?
25. what a big bear it is!
26. the bear has a cub

A doctor who takes care of animals is called a *veterinarian.* They help to keep animals well. Veterinarians go to school for many years. They must read about all the things that make animals sick. Veterinarians also must write directions for taking care of animals. Would you like to be a veterinarian? You can start by learning to read and write very well.

Careers

Parts of Telling Sentences

You know that a telling sentence is a group of words that states a complete idea. Every telling sentence has two parts. Each part does a special job in the sentence. The two parts work together to tell a complete idea.

The **subject part** of a sentence names whom or what the sentence is about.

The **predicate part** of a sentence tells what action the subject part does.

• Read each sentence. What is the subject part? What is the predicate part?

The class | went to the circus.
The children | saw many things.
The ponies | raced around the ring.
Lions | roared.
The clowns | jumped out of a tiny car.

Talk About It

Read each sentence. Is the part in the box the
subject part or the predicate part?

1. The class | watched a magic show.
2. A flower | turned into a white rabbit.
3. The white rabbit | turned into a bird.
4. The bird | flew away.

Skills Practice

Read each sentence. Look at the part in the box.
Write **subject** if it is a subject part. Write **predicate**
if it is a predicate part.

1. The children | saw a funny circus act.
2. A clown | brought some monkeys into the ring.
3. A red monkey | took the clown's hat.
4. A brown monkey | took the clown's shoes.
5. The funny clown | chased them.

Write each sentence. Draw a line between the
subject part and the predicate part.

6. Joe gave his pups a bath.
7. A pup splashed water.
8. The pup jumped out.
9. Joe ran after the pup.
10. The pup made tracks.
11. The children laughed.

Sample Answers 1. predicate 6. Joe | gave his pups a bath.

Building Sentences

You have learned about the two parts of a telling sentence. Every telling sentence has a subject part and a predicate part. The *subject part* names whom or what the sentence is about. The *predicate part* tells what action the subject part does.

Each part alone is not a sentence. It does not state a complete idea. You make a sentence when you join the subject part and the predicate part.

● Look at the subject parts and predicate parts below. Choose a subject part and a predicate part. Join the parts to make a sentence. Make as many sentences as you can using these parts.

SUBJECT PARTS	PREDICATE PARTS
The gray squirrel	dug a hole.
His friends	looked for nuts.
The squirrels	found many nuts.

Talk About It

Make a sentence using each of these subject parts. What part do you need to add?

1. The children ___ .   **2.** The little turtle ___ .

Make a sentence using each of these predicate parts. What part do you need to add?

3. ___ rode a horse.   **4.** ___ climbed a tree.

Skills Practice

Join each subject part with a predicate part. Write the sentences you have made.

1. The birds   paint in red.
2. The children   feed them.
3. Jay and Bonita   ride bicycles.
4. Other children   sing a song.
5. The happy birds   build a house for them.
6. Two dogs   live in the tree.
7. Three cats   run around the tree.
8. The sisters   sit in the sun.

Writing Sentences

Add a predicate part or a subject part to complete each sentence. Write the sentences.

1. Leslie ___ .   **4.** ___ drank milk.
2. The girls ___ .   **5.** ___ went to sleep.
3. An owl ___ .   **6.** ___ watched us play.

More Building Sentences

You have probably noticed that some telling sentences are very short.

Read these sentences.

A storm arrived.   The deer watched.

These are complete sentences. Both sentences have a subject part and a predicate part. But you can make these sentences tell more. You can add words to the subject part.

A sudden storm │ arrived.

A fierce storm │ arrived.

The words *sudden* and *fierce* tell more about *storm*. They help to build a more interesting subject part.

Sometimes you add words to the predicate part. These words can help your sentence tell more.

Read each sentence. What is added to the predicate part in each sentence? How does each predicate part help the sentence to tell more?

The deer │ watched the sky.

The deer │ watched anxiously.

The deer │ watched from the forest.

Talk About It

Read each sentence. Add more words to the subject part to make a good sentence.

1. Clouds gathered.
2. Trees shook.
3. Rabbits hopped.
4. Lightning flashed.

Read each sentence. Add more words to the predicate part to make a good sentence.

5. Thunder crashed.
6. Birds flew.
7. A raccoon watched.
8. Leaves fell.

Skills Practice

Add words to the subject part of each sentence. Then write the sentence.

1. The wind raged.
2. The animals waited.
3. A squirrel hid.
4. Streams flooded.
5. Chipmunks ran.
6. The storm ended.
7. The sun returned.
8. Bees buzzed.

Add words to the predicate part of each sentence. Then write the sentence.

9. Our family camped.
10. We explored.
11. Luis climbed.
12. Blueberries grew.
13. My uncle fished.
14. I swam.
15. Rob cooked.
16. We picnicked.

Skills Review

Read each sentence. Look at the part in the box. Write **subject** if it is a subject part. Write **predicate** if it is a predicate part.

1. Kay | walked across the meadow.
2. A rabbit | scurried by.
3. Kay | followed the rabbit.
4. The rabbit | hopped into the bushes.
5. Kay | looked all around.
6. Kay | found the rabbit with its family.

Write each sentence. Draw a line between the subject part and the predicate part.

7. Barry had a pet dragon.
8. The dragon liked blueberry pancakes.
9. Barry picked some blueberries.
10. The pet dragon made the pancakes.
11. The friends ate the pancakes.

Make some sentences. Join each subject part with a predicate part. Write the sentences.

12. Pam   walked to the store.
13. Her sister   saved her money.
14. The girls   bought a present.
15. The family   opened the present.
16. Mother   sang a song.

Add words to the subject part of each sentence.
Then write the sentence.

17. Horses trotted.
18. The puppy rolled over.
19. Our kitten climbed the tree.
20. The robins flew to the nest.
21. Tadpoles swam quickly.
22. The mouse took the cheese.

Add words to the predicate part of each sentence.
Then write the sentence.

23. Fish swam.
24. Our dog jumped.
25. The frog hopped.
26. Monkeys climbed.
27. Two bear cubs played.
28. The huge crocodile snapped.

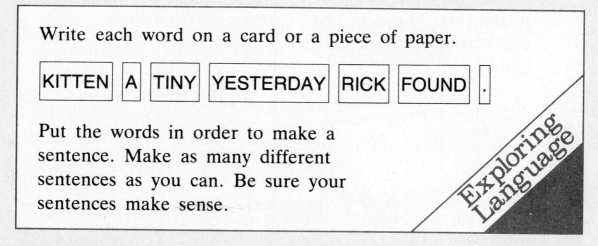

Write each word on a card or a piece of paper.

| KITTEN | A | TINY | YESTERDAY | RICK | FOUND | . |

Put the words in order to make a
sentence. Make as many different
sentences as you can. Be sure your
sentences make sense.

Exploring
Language

Parts of a Book

Most school books have more than one part. It is easier to use a book when you know how to use the parts.

The *table of contents* is at the front of the book. It lists what is in the book from beginning to end. It tells the number and name of each unit or chapter. It also tells on what page each unit or chapter begins. You can use the table of contents to learn about the book.

CONTENTS *PAGE*

The *index* is at the back of the book. It lists all the things that are in the book as well as the page numbers on which they appear. It is in alphabetical order. The index helps you find things quickly.

INDEX

Sometimes a book may have special parts before the index. Look at the back of this book. A special part called the Handbook begins on page 298. You can use the *handbook* to find important rules about your language.

Talk About It

Use this book to answer these questions.

1. How many units are in this book?
2. On what page does the first page of Unit 3 begin?
3. What is the name of the first lesson in Unit 4?
4. On what page does the index begin?
5. What is listed first in the index?
6. What is listed first in the handbook?

Skills Practice

Use the Table of Contents on page 18 to answer these questions. Write the answers.

1. What is the book about?
2. What is the name of Chapter 5?
3. Which chapter begins on page 15?
4. Is there a chapter about rabbits?
5. On what page does the index begin?

Use the Index on page 18 to answer these questions. Write the answers.

6. What pages tell about sharks?
7. What pages tell about turtles?
8. What page tells about salmon?

Learning About Paragraphs

You know how to write a sentence. A sentence is a group of words that states a complete idea.

Sometimes it takes more than one sentence to tell or explain something. Then you need to use a group of sentences.

A **paragraph** is a group of sentences that tells about one main idea.

The sentences in a paragraph must work together. The first sentence in a paragraph often states the most important idea of the paragraph. This sentence is called the *main idea sentence*. The other sentences tell more about the main idea. They are called *detail sentences*.

A **main idea sentence** states the most important idea of the paragraph.

Detail sentences tell more about the main idea.

- Read this paragraph about Donna and her cat. What is the main idea sentence? What are the detail sentences?

Donna takes good care of her cat. First she feeds the cat. Next she plays with the cat. Then she brushes the cat.

Did you find the main idea sentence in the paragraph about Donna? Did you find the details? Here is a way to see how they work together.

Main idea: Donna takes good care of her cat.
  Detail 1: First she feeds the cat.
  Detail 2: Next she plays with the cat.
  Detail 3: Then she brushes the cat.

Talk About It

Read this paragraph. What is the main idea sentence? What are the detail sentences?

Two robins raised a family in our tree. First the mother robin laid four eggs in a nest. Then she sat on them. Now the robins have four noisy babies.

Skills Practice

Write these labels on your paper.

Main Idea:
    Detail 1:
    Detail 2:
    Detail 3:

Read this paragraph. Fill in the main idea and details on your paper.

Our class raised some frogs. First we got some frog eggs. Then the eggs grew into tadpoles. At last the tadpoles became baby frogs.

Time Order in Paragraphs

Thinking About Paragraphs

You know that the words in a sentence must be in an order that makes sense. The sentences in a paragraph must also be in an order that makes sense.

Here is one good way to arrange the sentences in a paragraph.

1. Start with a main idea sentence. This sentence tells what the paragraph will be about.

2. Add detail sentences to tell more about the main idea. Put your detail sentences in *time order*. Tell what happened *first*. Tell what happened *next*. Tell what happened *last*.

● Read this paragraph about Mr. Paso.

Mr. Paso works in a pet shop. First he opens the store. Next he feeds the pets. Then he cleans their cages. Last he lets us play with the pets.

The first sentence tells the main idea of the paragraph. It tells about Mr. Paso's job in a pet shop. The detail sentences are in time order. They tell what he does first, next, and last. They are in an order that makes sense.

Look at the first word in the paragraph about Mr. Paso's job. It is moved in a little space from the left margin. It is *indented*. Indenting helps the reader know where a new paragraph begins. Indent the first word of a paragraph.

Talking About Paragraphs

Read these detail sentences. They are not in time order. Put them in a time order that makes sense.

1. a. Later the chipmunk ran home with the nut.
   b. First the chipmunk looked around carefully.
   c. Next the chipmunk picked up the big nut.

Read these sentences. They tell about one idea. Choose the main idea sentence. Then put the detail sentences in a time order that makes sense.

2. a. First Kevin slipped on the ice.
   b. Next Father took him to the doctor.
   c. Kevin broke his arm.
   d. Now Kevin wears a cast on his broken arm.

Writing a Paragraph

Read these sentences. They tell about one idea. Choose the main idea sentence. Then put the detail sentences in a time order that makes sense. Write the paragraph. Remember to indent the first word.

   a. Last she put the pots in a sunny window.
   b. Jane started a window garden.
   c. Then she watered the seeds.
   d. First she filled some pots with dirt and seeds.

A Class Paragraph

Thinking About Paragraphs

Your class is going to write a paragraph together. The pictures will help you. They show how Bert fixed a bed for his new puppy. The pictures are in the right time order to make sense.

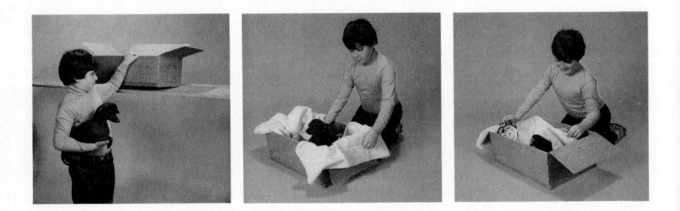

Writing a Paragraph

1. Your paragraph will start with a main idea sentence. The main idea sentence is *Bert made a bed for his new puppy.* Your teacher will write it on the board.

2. Think of a detail sentence that tells about the first picture. Your teacher will write it on the board.

3. Think of detail sentences for the next two pictures. Your teacher will write them.

4. Copy the paragraph on your paper. Remember to indent the first word.

Practicing A Time Order Paragraph

Thinking About Your Paragraph

Now you are going to write your own paragraph. The pictures will help you. They show how George built a birdhouse.

The Word Bank will help you, too. It shows how to spell some of the words you may want to use.

Writing Your Paragraph

Word Bank

first
next
then
last
boards
father
hammer
nail
paint
green

1. Your paragraph should start with a main idea sentence. The main idea sentence is *George built a birdhouse*. Write this sentence on your paper. Remember to indent the first word.

2. Look at the first picture. Write a detail sentence that tells about the picture. Use your Word Bank to help you spell your words.

3. Write a detail sentence about the next picture.

4. Now write a detail sentence about the last picture.

5. Save your paragraph.

How To Edit Your Work

After you write a paragraph, it is a good idea to edit it. Edit means "to read carefully and fix any mistakes." Check for these things:

First be sure your paragraph says what you want it to say.

1. Does the main idea sentence tell what the paragraph is about?
2. Are your detail sentences in a time order that makes sense?
3. Does each sentence state a complete idea?

Next be sure other people can read your paragraph.

4. Did you indent the first word?
5. Did you begin each sentence with a capital letter and end it with a period?
6. Did you spell all the words correctly?

Remember to use your Word Bank.

Read Jane's paragraph. What mistakes did Jane make? How did she correct them?

¶I went to the zoo last Sunday.
First
first I saw some lions and tigers.
Next I saw a baby giraffe. Then I
Last
got some peanuts. I fed some
monkeys
of them to the moneys.

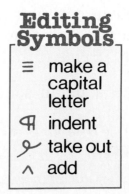

Editing Symbols

≡ make a capital letter

¶ indent

✎ take out

∧ add

Edit Your Paragraph

Edit your paragraph about George's birdhouse. Use the check questions and editing symbols on page 26 to correct your mistakes. Make a good copy of your paragraph.

A Time Order Paragraph in a Diary

Prewriting Many people keep diaries. A diary records what happens to a person every day. Suppose you kept a diary. Think about what happened to you yesterday. What did you do in the morning, afternoon, and evening? As you remember things, jot down words or notes that tell what happened to you yesterday.

Writing Write a paragraph for your diary that tells about yesterday. Start your paragraph with a main idea sentence. Then look at your notes to write your detail sentences.

Editing Use the check questions and the editing symbols on page 26 to edit the paragraph for your diary.

Unit Review

Read the groups of words in each pair. Write each
group of words that is a sentence. *pages 2-3*

1. The horse eats hay.
   The horse.

2. A cow.
   A cow gives milk.

3. Some pigs roll in mud.
   Some pigs.

4. The chickens lay eggs.
   The chickens.

Read each sentence. Write **telling** if it is a telling
sentence. Write **question** if it is a question sentence.
Write **exclamation** if it is an exclamation sentence. *pages 4-5*

5. Did you see the monkeys?
6. They were in the trees.
7. Two monkeys hung by their tails.
8. What funny monkeys they were!

Some special signs are missing in each sentence.
Write each sentence correctly. *pages 6-7*

9. our class has a gerbil.
10. Who feeds the gerbil
11. how quickly the gerbil runs
12. it is fun to watch the gerbil

Read each sentence. Look at the part in the box.
Write **subject** if it is a subject part. Write **predicate**
if it is a predicate part. *pages 10-13*

13. The bear │climbed to the top of the tree.
14. The baby robins │ chirped loudly.

15. The snake | moved from beneath the rocks.
16. The alligators | rested on the river bank.
17. The horse | trotted down the path.

Add words to the subject part of each sentence.
Then write the sentence. *pages 14–15*

18. The birds sang.   20. The kittens played.
19. The dog barks.   21. The bear climbs.

Add words to the predicate part of each sentence.
Then write the sentence. *pages 14–15*

22. The rabbit ate.   24. The lion roars.
23. The cat scratched.   25. The fox watches.

Read these detail sentences. They are not in time
order. Write them in a time order that makes sense. *pages 22–23*

26. a. Next we painted the house bright green.
    b. Last we put food inside for the birds.
    c. First we built a bird house out of wood.

Read these sentences. Choose the main idea
sentence. Then put the detail sentences in a time
order that makes sense. Write the paragraph. *pages 22–23*

27. a. Then the family drove to the picnic area.
    b. First they made the food for the picnic.
    c. Ming's family went on a picnic on Sunday.
    d. Last everyone sat on the ground and ate.

Do you have a favorite place to play by yourself? It may be a secret place that no one else knows about.

In this story a boy takes you to his secret places. They are in the woods near his house. He tells about his secret places in order. First he talks about people who lived in the woods. Then he talks about the woods today. Last he tells about something new in the woods.

You may find some new words in this story in *Words to Think About*. They will help you understand the story.

Words to Think About

settlers, people who make a home in a new place

olden days, a long time ago

meadow, a field of grass

Secret Places

I have a secret place in the woods I call Old Log Cabin. Settlers built it in the olden days. They lived here, they ate here, and at night they slept here. There aren't any more settlers, but there were. Now there are only woods, lots of woods.

I have a secret place in the woods I call The Fishing Hole. Frogs hop by it, water splashes into it, and fish swim in it. There aren't many fish, there are only some. But there are woods, lots of woods.

I have a secret place in the woods I call
The Forest. I dance here, I climb here, I
run here, and I play here. The woods are
the prettiest place I know. And there are
woods, lots of woods.

I have a secret place I call The
Meadow. Grasshoppers hop here, flowers
grow here, crickets chirp here, and birds
sing here, in the woods, in all the woods.

I know another place in the woods. It has no name. Diggers dig there, trucks drive there, houses grow there, and people work there. I hope they never find my secret places.

D. J. Arneson

Creative Activities

1. **Creative Writing** Imagine a secret place that only you know about. Write a paragraph that tells what your secret place looks like, or write a paragraph that tells what you like to do there.

2. Think about your secret places. Draw pictures of some of them. Show what you like to do in each place. Put the pictures in the order that you like to visit the places.

3. Pretend you are a bug with a secret place in your classroom. Tell how to get from your secret place to the door of the room. See if your classmates can guess the secret place.

OLD TRAIN ENGINE AT STRASBURG, PENNSYLVANIA

Grammar and Related Language Skills

Nouns
Singular and Plural Nouns
Proper and Common Nouns
Commas in Addresses and Dates

Practical Communication

STUDY AND REFERENCE SKILLS
Using a Dictionary

COMPOSITION
Writing a Description Paragraph

Creative Expression

Poetry

2

If you could travel on a train, where would you want to go? People who travel make many plans in advance. Travelers must make travel and hotel reservations. Some travelers plan to contact friends or relatives in the places they visit. What other plans might a traveler make? What speaking and writing skills would help a traveler?

Learning About Nouns

You know that a sentence states a complete idea. Now you will learn about words that help state ideas in sentences.

> A **noun** is a word that names a
> person, a place, or a thing.

Kate and Eric took a bus trip last summer. The picture shows some people, places, and things that they saw.

- Name some *people* Kate and Eric saw. Name the *place* shown in the picture. Name some *things* that Kate and Eric saw. The people, places, and things that you named are all nouns. What other people, places, and things do you think Kate and Eric saw on their trip?

- Read each of these sentences. Why is the word in the box a noun?

I took a bus to Topeka. The bus traveled very fast.

My mother went, too. I saw many buildings.

Talk About It

Read each sentence. Then read the nouns.

1. Meg got in the car.
2. A woman rode on the bus.
3. The streets were very bumpy in Centertown.
4. The girl visited her grandmother.

Skills Practice

Read each sentence. Write the nouns.

1. Mike flew in an airplane.
2. A girl sat nearby.
3. Her friend wore glasses.
4. A man waved from the ground.
5. A strong wind blew in his face.
6. The boy landed in St. Louis.

Writing Sentences

Pretend you visited a big city. Tell what you saw.

1. Write a sentence with a noun that names a person.
2. Write a sentence with a noun that names a place.
3. Write a sentence with a noun that names a thing.

Sample Answer 1. Mike, airplane

Nouns in Sentences

You use nouns almost every time you make sentences. Some nouns are in the subject part of a sentence. To find nouns in the subject part, remember these two things.

A **noun** is a word that names a person, a place, or a thing.

The **subject part** of a sentence names whom or what the sentence is about.

• Look at the subject part of each sentence. Read each noun.

The **gate** closed in front of us.

A long **train** raced by.

The **engineer** blew the whistle.

Sometimes nouns are in the predicate part of a sentence. Remember,

The **predicate part** of a sentence tells what action the subject part does.

• Look at the predicate part of each sentence. Is there a noun in the predicate part? What is it?

Rosalie rode on a **train** .

The engine chugged .

The train went to **Chicago** .

Talk About It

Read these sentences. What are the nouns in the subject parts? What are the nouns in the predicate parts?

1. Many people hurried through the station .
2. A boy carried two bags .
3. Nadia got on the train .

Skills Practice

Write each sentence. Draw a line under each noun.

1. The children rode on the train.
2. Henry ran to the first car.
3. Isabel sat next to a window.
4. The whistle blew.
5. Cows watched the train pass.
6. Pete ate apples for lunch.
7. Rick visited the engine.

Writing Sentences

Pretend you are riding a train. Think of a noun for each blank. Write each sentence.

1. Our trip took us to ____ .
2. A ____ took a picture of the train.
3. The ____ made noise all night.
4. ____ wrote letters to ____ .

Sample Answer 1. The <u>children</u> rode on the <u>train</u>.

Singular and Plural Nouns

Some nouns name only one person, place, or thing. Other nouns name more than one person, place, or thing.

> A **singular noun** is a noun that names one person, place, or thing.
> pirate   sea   ship

> A **plural noun** is a noun that names more than one person, place, or thing.
> pirates   seas   ships

Singular and plural nouns have different forms. The form shows if the noun names one or more than one.

- Look at the forms of the nouns in each box. Which nouns are singular? Which nouns are plural?

| car | driver | town |
| cars | drivers | towns |

The plural nouns in the boxes end with *s*.

- Look at the picture below. Which card belongs under each picture? Why?

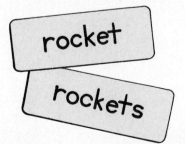

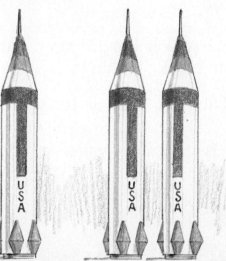

Talk About It

Choose the noun that belongs in the blank in each sentence. Tell if it is singular or plural.

1. Three ___ rode on their bikes. (boy, boys)
2. One ___ got a flat tire. (bike, bikes)
3. Another bike hit many ___ . (rock, rocks)
4. This bike has two flat ___ . (tire, tires)
5. They could not ride on one ___ . (bike, bikes)
6. The three ___ returned home. (boy, boys)

Skills Practice

Write each noun. Then write **singular** if the noun is singular. Write **plural** if the noun is plural.

1. dog   4. table   7. uncle
2. kittens   5. pond   8. cups
3. chairs   6. aunts   9. duck

Write each sentence with the correct noun.

10. Karen went for a ___ . (walk, walks)
11. Many of her ___ joined her. (friend, friends)
12. All the ___ met at the park. (girl, girls)
13. They hiked for two ___ . (mile, miles)
14. Sara lost a ___ along the way. (shoe, shoes)
15. It fell near a ___ . (stream, streams)
16. The girls looked for ten ___ . (minute, minutes)
17. A ___ found the shoe. (friend, friends)

Sample Answers **1.** dog, singular **10.** Karen went for a walk.

Forming Plural Nouns

Singular nouns name one person, place, or thing. Plural nouns name more than one person, place, or thing. You can make a singular noun into a plural noun by changing the form of the word.

To make most singular nouns plural, add an **-s.**

- Read each pair of nouns. Does each noun name one or more than one? Is each noun singular or plural? What was added to each singular noun to make it plural?

truck	bridge	garage	mountain
trucks	bridges	garages	mountains

Sometimes you have to add *-es* to make a singular noun plural.

If a singular noun ends with **s, ss, x, ch,** or **sh,** add **-es** to write the plural.

- Read each pair of nouns. Does each noun name one or more than one? Is each noun singular or plural? What was added to each singular noun to make the plural form?

bus	dress	box	branch	dish
buses	dresses	boxes	branches	dishes

Sometimes you have to change the spelling of a noun before you add *-es* to make it plural.

If a singular noun ends with a **consonant** and **y,** change **y** to **i** and add **-es** to write the plural.

baby

babi + es $\longrightarrow$ babies

- Look at each pair of nouns. How is the spelling changed to make the plural form?

country	city	penny
countries	cities	pennies

Talk About It

Spell the plural of each noun.

1. party	**4.** family	**7.** puppy	**10.** baby
2. tree	**5.** dress	**8.** clock	**11.** dish
3. fox	**6.** shirt	**9.** ranch	**12.** class

Skills Practice

Write the plural of each noun.

1. bunny	**4.** window	**7.** car	**10.** country
2. blueberry	**5.** door	**8.** cherry	**11.** crow
3. bus	**6.** city	**9.** wish	**12.** fly

Writing Sentences

Read the words below. Write four sentences. In each sentence, use the plural of one of these words.

pony   splash   toy   story

Sample Answer **1.** bunnies

More Plural Nouns

You already know how to write the plural of most nouns. Some singular nouns form the plural in a different way. You have to learn the plural of these nouns.

- Look at each noun below.

tooth ⟶ teeth   child ⟶ children
ox ⟶ oxen   goose ⟶ geese
man ⟶ men   mouse ⟶ mice
foot ⟶ feet   woman ⟶ women

Talk About It

Read each sentence. At the end of each sentence is a singular noun. Say the plural of the noun.

1. Two ___ swam in the pond.   (goose)
2. All three ___ are doctors.   (woman)
3. Both of José's ___ hurt.   (foot)
4. A team of ___ pulled the cart.   (ox)

Skills Practice

Write the plural of these nouns.

1. man   5. foot
2. goose   6. ox
3. tooth   7. child
4. woman   8. mouse

Sample Answer 1. men

Making New Words

You can make new words from some words you already know. One way of making new words is to add *-er* to the end of certain words. Each new word tells what kind of work a person does.

- Look at each pair of words.

climb   print
climb**er**   print**er**

Someone who <u>climbs</u> is   Someone who <u>prints</u> is
a <u>climber</u>.   a <u>printer</u>.

Talk About It

Look at the underlined word. Change it into a word to tell what kind of work the person does. Your answer should make sense in the blank.

1. Mr. Caplan <u>teaches</u> school.   **2.** Ms. Janson <u>drives</u> a bus.
Mr. Caplan is a ____ .   Ms. Janson is a bus ____ .

Skills Practice

Look at the underlined word in each pair of sentences. Change it into a word to tell what kind of work the person does. Write the sentence.

1. Bob <u>plays</u> baseball.   **3.** Mrs. Kato <u>reports</u> the news.
   Bob is a baseball ____ .   Mrs. Kato is a news ____ .

2. Ellen <u>writes</u> stories.   **4.** Mr. Como <u>builds</u> houses.
Ellen is a ____ .   Mr. Como is a ____ .

Sample Answer 1. Bob is a baseball player.

Skills Review

Read each sentence. Write the nouns.

1. The children borrow books from the library.
2. The woman walked quickly.
3. Mr. Johnson drove the children to school.
4. Carlos ran along the road.
5. The dogs played with the ball.
6. My mother works in a bank.
7. The boys raced home.

Write each sentence. Draw a line under each noun.

8. Ms. Clark picked the apples.
9. A robin landed on the ground.
10. Joey watched the game.
11. The car honked.
12. The bus stopped by the tree.
13. The babies drank the milk.
14. Many people enjoy the park.

Write each noun. Then write **singular** if the noun is singular. Write **plural** if the noun is plural.

15. pitcher   18. cat   21. streets   24. shoe
16. brooks   19. wishes   22. ranch   25. foxes
17. day   20. river   23. frogs   26. pennies

Write the correct noun for each sentence.

27. Some children visited a ____ . (park, parks)
28. Five ____ played on the swings. (girl, girls)

29. Three ___ hunted for bugs. (boy, boys)

30. The boys caught two ___ . (fly, flies)

31. The children ate lunch under a ___ . (tree, trees)

32. Two ___ drove through the park. (bus, buses)

33. Sally found a ___ on the ground. (dollar, dollars)

34. She put the money in a ___ . (pocket, pockets)

Write the plural of each noun.

35. wagon	**39.** story	**43.** dish
36. room	**40.** city	**44.** ox
37. toy	**41.** rabbit	**45.** foot
38. glass	**42.** family	**46.** mouse

Look at the underlined word. Change it into a
word that tells what kind of work the person does.
Write the new word.

47. Amy <u>trains</u> animals.
Amy is an animal ___ .

48. Roy <u>farms</u> the land.
Roy is a ___ .

49. Leroy <u>skates</u> on ice.
Leroy is an ice ___ .

50. Betty <u>climbs</u> mountains.
Betty is a mountain ___ .

Make as many nouns as
you can. You can use only
the letters in this noun:

astronaut

Exploring Language

Proper and Common Nouns

You know that a noun names a person, place, or thing. Some nouns name special people, places, and things.

> A **common noun** is a noun that names any person, place, or thing.

> A **proper noun** is a noun that names a special person, place, or thing.

May has five turtles. Here are their names.

Rocky   King   Snappy   Bowser   Snoop

When May says the word *turtle,* she could be talking about any turtle. The word *turtle* is a common noun. When she says the word *Snappy,* you know she is talking about a special turtle. *Snappy* is a proper noun.

- Read each pair of nouns. Which is a common noun? Which is a proper noun?

Susan	boy	Hill School
girl	Paul Ramos	school
city	Alaska	statue
San Francisco	state	Statue of Liberty

Many proper nouns have more than one word.

> Begin each important word in a proper noun with a capital letter.

● Look again at the proper nouns in the box. Which words begin with capital letters?

Talk About It

Look at the nouns that are underlined. Tell whether each noun is a proper noun or a common noun.

1. A <u>woman</u> climbed <u>Mount Ap</u>.
2. <u>Snow</u> covered the <u>mountain</u>.
3. The <u>top</u> was in the <u>clouds</u>.
4. A <u>man</u> wrote about her <u>trip</u>.

Skills Practice

1. Find the proper nouns in the box. Write them.
2. Find the common nouns in the box. Write them.

baseball	Empire State Building	Johnny Appleseed
mountain	apple	city
Dayton	Toronto Blue Jays	Rocky Mountains

Write each noun. Write **proper** if it is a proper noun. Write **common** if it is a common noun.

3. The boy lives near Forest Park.
4. Carlos Rivera skates at the park.
5. Myra rides her bike.
6. The children from Webster School visit in April.
7. Many people have picnics in the park.
8. Jean walks home on Elm Street.

Sample Answer 3. boy, common, Forest Park, proper

Writing Proper Nouns

All people have names. Their names are proper nouns. There is a special way to write proper nouns that name people.

- Look at the picture. What are the names of the children? Are the names proper nouns?

Sometimes people use initials instead of their full names.

An **initial** is the first letter of a name.
Write an initial with a capital letter.
Put a period after the letter.

- Look at these ways of writing the same name. How are initials used in each one?

Thomas Adam Cantor   Thomas A. Cantor
T. A. Cantor   T. A. C.

- Look at the picture. How would you use initials to write the names of the children?

Some people use titles in front of their names.

Begin a **title** with a capital letter.
End most titles with a period.

● Read the titles in these names. Which of these titles does not end with a period?

Dr. Lisa Jones   Mrs. Ann Ramirez   Ms. Leslie Zhan

Mr. Albert Penson   Miss Jane Costa

Talk About It

How would you write each of these names?

1. mrs robertson
2. miss masters

3. mr mark m jensen
4. dr carla boone

Skills Practice

Write each name correctly.

1. mrs d silver
2. mr cramer

3. linda l stevens
4. dr michael koval

Write each sentence correctly.

5. Did tommy ryan tell you?
6. Our class gave mr walker a party.
7. We invited dr anders to come.
8. I helped sandy rosen make lemonade.
9. P j carlin read a story by laura ingalls wilder.

Writing Sentences

Write two sentences about yourself.

1. Use your full name in a sentence.
2. Use your initials in a sentence.

Sample Answers 1. Mrs. D. Silver **5.** Did Tommy Ryan tell you?

Commas in Addresses and Dates

You know that proper nouns can name special people. Each name begins with a capital letter. Now you will learn how to write names of special places and days.

Use **capital letters** to begin proper nouns that name places.

- Find the proper nouns in this picture. What do they name?

The names of streets begin with capital letters.

Spring Street   Elm Road

The names of cities and states begin with capital letters.

Greenburg   Ohio

Put a **comma** (,) between the name of the city and the state when you write them together.

Greenburg, Ohio

Sometimes you need to show where someone lives.

An **address** shows where someone lives.

An address shows the house number, the name of the street, the city, the state, and the ZIP code. It is often written with a person's name. Each proper noun in an address begins with a capital letter.

Sometimes you need to write the date. You use a comma between the day of the month and the year.

Use a **comma** (,) to separate the day of the month from the year.

April 7, 1981   October 30, 1982

Talk About It

How should each of these names and dates be written?

1. oak street   **4.** gary indiana   **7.** June 4 1983

2. orangetown   **5.** weston vermont   **8.** August 22 1981

3. mill avenue   **6.** dallas texas   **9.** May 13 1981

Skills Practice

Write each name and address correctly.

1. dr jan mills
36 adams street
chicago illinois 60607

2. mr sam henson
615 rabbit road
sun city arizona 85351

Write each date correctly.

3. April 10 1982   **6.** October 8 1983

4. August 13 1980   **7.** January 30 1982

5. February 6 1981   **8.** December 23 1984

Skills Review

Write each noun. Write **proper** if it is a proper noun. Write **common** if it is a common noun.

1. The woman helped build Peachtree Center.
2. Joe Turner works at the station.
3. The boy goes to Lakeland School.
4. The children visited the San Diego Zoo.
5. A girl saw the squirrel.
6. The man drove along Ocean Avenue.
7. Bob Walker got into the car.

Write each sentence correctly. Make sure you write each name correctly.

8. Gail goldberg went to the library.
9. Mr teller read stories by r l jones.
10. Then ms b a kaywood sang a song.
11. Dr j k martin helped mrs anita lind with the food.
12. We visited miss rose w carter.

Write each name and address correctly.

13.
```
don ito
47 mountain avenue
denver colorado 80220
```

14.
```
mr manuel gomez
54 orange road
somerset kentucky 42501
```

15.

> ms dora williams
> 21 main street
> redkey indiana 47373

16.

> dr kim wu
> 2 forest road
> fargo north dakota 58102

Write each date correctly.

17. January 1 1936

18. May 30 1922

19. March 8 1963

20. October 24 1975

21. December 30 1976

22. November 6 1981

In early times, people were known by the kind of work they did. In a small town, there might be a few men named Jack. To make clear which person they were talking about, they would say *Jack the Miller* or *Jack the Miner*. In time, they became Jack Miller and Jack Miner. Think of some other names that might have come about in the same way.

Exploring Language

Dictionary: Alphabetical Order

When you read, you may find words that are new to you. You may want to learn how to spell words. You can find out more about words by using a dictionary.

All the words in a dictionary are written in alphabetical order. *Alphabetical order* means that words are placed in the same order as the letters of the alphabet. You must know how to use alphabetical order to use the dictionary.

A B C D E F G H I J K L M N O P Q R S T U V W X Y Z

Here is a list of words. Look at the first letter of each word. These letters come in the same order as the letters of the alphabet. So these words are in alphabetical order.

> fox
> **m**an
> **r**ing

- Look at the three words in each list. Are they in alphabetical order?

ask	door	win
boy	play	toy
car	zoo	song

Here is another list of words. All these words begin with the same letter. Look at the second letter of each word. These letters come in the same order as the letters of the alphabet. So these words are in alphabetical order.

> clock
> come
> cut

• Look at the three words in each list. Are they in alphabetical order?

four	dance	milk	seeds
fish	deer	money	salt
from	drum	mule	soup

Talk About It

Put each list of three words in alphabetical order.

1. free
desk
hammer

2. question
invite
garage

3. noise
name
news

Skills Practice

Write each list of three words in alphabetical order.

1. cap
ant
bat

4. some
splash
score

7. under
up
use

2. block
beside
bird

5. apple
over
down

8. giant
school
goat

3. cold
huge
hear

6. mark
dragon
snow

9. eleven
engine
east

Sample Answer **1.** ant
bat
cap

Words That Describe Senses

Thinking About Words That Describe

You have five senses. They are seeing, hearing, smelling, tasting, and touching. Your senses help you to know the world around you. Words that describe senses can make things come alive in your mind. They help you know how something sounds or looks. They also may help you know how something tastes, feels, or smells.

- Read each sentence. Which sense does each underlined word make you think of?

Mark found a <u>shiny</u> coin.   <u>Booming</u> thunder scared us.
An <u>icy</u> wind chilled me.   I like <u>sour</u> pickles.

You can use sense words in a special way. You can use them to *compare* two different things. When you compare, you show how two different things are alike. You often use the words *like* or *as* when you compare.

- Read each sentence. How are the two underlined words compared? Which sense helps you to understand each sentence?

The <u>stone</u> was as smooth as <u>glass</u>.
The twinkling <u>lights</u> glittered like <u>stars</u>.
The <u>fruit</u> was as sweet as <u>honey</u>.

Talking About Words That Describe

Think of a word to complete each sentence.

1. My toes felt as cold as ____ .
2. Joy was as quiet as a ____ .
3. The snowflakes sparkled like ____ .
4. My hat is as soft as ____ .
5. The cookie is as hard as a ____ .
6. His voice boomed like ____ .

Writing Words That Describe

Think of a word to complete each sentence.
Then write the sentence.

1. The wind howled like a ____ .
2. My jeans are as stiff as ____ .
3. The burned soup smelled like ____ .
4. The water is as clear as ____ .
5. My voice squeaked like a ____ .
6. The apple was as sweet as ____ .
7. The snow crunched like ____ .
8. The hot peppers burned like ____ .
9. Ed was as pale as a ____ .
10. The new dress was as scratchy as ____ .

Write three sentences that compare two different
things. Use the word *like* or *as* in each sentence.

11. Write a sentence telling how <u>smooth</u> a thing is.
12. Write a sentence telling how <u>bright</u> a thing is.
13. Write a sentence telling what an old door <u>sounds</u> like.

Paragraphs That Describe

Thinking About Paragraphs

You can write paragraphs to tell about different things. One kind of paragraph tells what something is like. This kind of paragraph can tell how something looks. It can tell how something tastes or feels. It may even tell how something smells or sounds. This kind of paragraph describes something or someone.

• Read this paragraph. It describes a puppet.

> My puppet looks like Snow White. She has brown buttons for eyes. Her hair is made from black wool. She wears a dress made from red cloth. Her dress feels very soft.

Talking About Paragraphs

1. What is the main idea sentence in the paragraph?

2. Which detail sentences tell what the puppet looks like?

3. Which detail sentence tells what the dress feels like?

4. How do you think the puppet sounds?

5. Now you have read about the puppet. Can you draw a picture of the puppet?

A Class Paragraph

Now you can write a paragraph with your class. Look at the picture. It shows how Bobby dressed on Halloween. Write a paragraph to describe how he dressed. Your teacher will write all your sentences on the board.

1. The main idea sentence is *Bobby wore a pirate costume on Halloween.* Your teacher will write it on the board.

2. Look at the picture of Bobby's costume. Think of a detail sentence to describe his hat. Your teacher will write it on the board.

3. Think of a detail sentence to describe his coat.

4. Now look at his face. Think of a detail sentence to describe it.

5. Read your paragraph. Does it describe how Bobby dressed?

6. Copy the paragraph on your paper. Be sure to indent the first word.

Practicing a Descriptive Paragraph

Thinking About Your Paragraph

Now you can write your own paragraph. Pretend you got a new puppy. Write a paragraph describing your new puppy. You may want to use some of the words in the Word Bank.

Writing Your Paragraph

1. Write this main idea sentence on your paper. *I have a new puppy named Lucky.* Remember to indent the first word.

2. Write a detail sentence to tell how big Lucky is. Use the Word Bank to help you spell your words.

3. Write a detail sentence to tell what color Lucky is.

4. Write two other detail sentences that compare Lucky to something. Use *like* or *as* in each sentence.

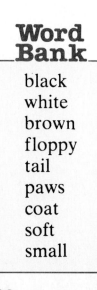

Word Bank

black
white
brown
floppy
tail
paws
coat
soft
small

Edit Your Paragraph

Read your paragraph again. Think about these questions as you read.

Editing Symbols

≡ make a capital letter

¶ indent

⌇ take out

∧ add

1. Does each detail sentence describe the main idea?
2. What nouns did you use?
3. Did you begin each proper noun with a capital letter?
4. Did you indent the first word?
5. Did you spell all the words correctly?

Correct your mistakes. If you need to, write your paragraph again.

INDEPENDENT WRITING

A Descriptive Paragraph

Prewriting Writing a describing paragraph is like drawing a picture. You use words instead of paint or crayons. Think about a friend. Jot down some words or notes that answer these questions: What colors are your friend's eyes and hair? How tall is your friend? What is your friend's favorite game? What else will you write about your friend?

Writing Write a paragraph that describes your friend. Start your paragraph with a main idea sentence that names your friend. Then use the answers to the questions to write the sentences that describe your friend.

Editing Use the check questions and editing symbols above to edit your paragraph.

Unit Review

Read each sentence. Write the nouns. *pages 36-39*

1. The girl rows a boat.
2. Two boys fish from the dock.
3. Many people sail on the big ship.
4. A woman waves from the deck.

Write each sentence with the correct noun. *pages 40-41*

5. My friend pulled a red ___ . (wagon, wagons)
6. Two ___ rode in it. (kitten, kittens)
7. They slept in a straw ___ . (basket, baskets)
8. Three ___ saw the kittens. (girl, girls)
9. My brother wanted a ___ . (kitten, kittens)

Write the plural of each noun. *pages 42-44*

10. dress	12. country	14. foot
11. jet	13. bench	15. fox

Change the underlined word in each pair of sentences to tell what kind of work the person does. *page 45*

16. Mr. Black <u>teaches</u> school.
    Mr. Black is a ___ .

17. Rose <u>hikes</u> in the woods.
    Rose is a ___ .

18. You <u>play</u> hockey.
    You are a hockey ___ .

Write each noun. Write **proper** if it is a proper noun.
Write **common** if it is a common noun. *pages 48-49*

19. The children went to Florida.
20. Robin liked Disney World.
21. Simon swam at Miami Beach.
22. Dr. Ross took the train to New York.
23. The train stopped at Baltimore.

Write each name and address correctly. *pages 50-53*

24. ms isabel minsky
35 west end avenue
new york new york 10011

25. mr alonso pérez
18 green street
baker nevada 89311

Write each date correctly. *pages 52-53*

26. May 15 1926
27. June 6 1984
28. March 12 1982

29. June 3 1963
30. January 10 1983
31. February 12 1982

You are going to write a paragraph that
describes a cat. Here is the main idea
sentence: *Our new cat is beautiful.* You may
use these words in your detail sentences.
Write at least one detail sentence using
like or *as* to compare the cat to something. *pages 58-63*

| white |
| gray |
| yellow |
| glow |
| dark |
| tiny |

32. Write the main idea sentence of the paragraph.
33. Write a sentence that describes the cat's hair.
34. Write a sentence that describes the cat's eyes.
35. Write a sentence that describes the cat's feet.

A *poem* is a special way to paint pictures in words. When you read a poem, you can see pictures in your mind. The writer chooses each word carefully. The meaning of each word must fit the idea in the poem. These poems are about ways to travel. Your teacher will read each poem to you. Try to picture what the words describe.

BUS RIDE

I hailed the bus and I went for a ride
And I rode on top and not inside
As I'd done on every other day:

The air was so sweet and the city so gay
The sun was so hot and the air so mellow

And the shops were bursting with green and yellow.

The shops were the brightest I'd ever seen—
Full of yellow and pink and green,
Yellow in this and green in that,
A dress or a kerchief, a tie or a hat,

And I wanted to dance and I wanted to sing
And I bought a flower because it was spring.

Selma Robinson

Song of the Train

(*softly*)
Clickety-clack,
Wheels on the track,
This is the way
They begin the attack:

(*louder*)
Click-ety-clack,
Click-ety-clack.
Click-ety, *clack-ety,*
Click-ety,
Clack.

(*louder*)
Clickety-clack,
Over the crack,
Faster and faster
The song of the track:
Clickety-clack,
Clickety-clack,
Clickety, clackety,
Clackety,
Clack.

(*softly*)
Riding in front,
Riding in back,
Everyone hears
The song of the track:
Clickety-clack,
Clickety-clack,
Clickety, *clickety,*
Clackety,
Clack.

—*David McCord*

Creative Activities

1. In "Bus Ride" find words for colors and things to wear that add to the picture of spring. In "Song of the Train," what words sound like train noises?

2. **Creative Writing**   Think of interesting words to go in the blanks. Write the sentences. The first one is done for you.

   Lightning is like <u>a crack in the sky</u>.
   Sunshine is like_____.
   Thunder is like _____.

GYMNAST

Grammar and
Related Language Skills

Verbs
Verbs in the Present
Verbs in the Past
Spelling Verbs

Practical Communication

STUDY AND REFERENCE SKILLS
Following and Giving Directions
Using Test-Taking Skills
COMPOSITION
Writing a Direction Paragraph

Creative Expression

A Picture Story

Do you sing in a chorus or dance with a group of friends? Have you ever tried gymnastics? Students and teachers sometimes start special activity groups after school. What are some activities that interest you? What speaking and writing skills would help you start a recreation group? Why is recreation after school important?

Learning About Verbs

You do many things each day. Sometimes you want to tell someone about the things you do. Then you need to use words that name actions. Words like *skip* and *hop* name actions.

- Look at the picture.

  What action is the girl doing with the rope?
  What action is the boy doing with the ball?
  What action is the dog waiting to do?

  > A **verb** is a word that names an action.

- Read each sentence. What action does each verb name?

  Mark <u>hops</u> on one foot.   Paco <u>tosses</u> a ball.
  Jean <u>jumps</u> rope very fast.   His dog <u>catches</u> the ball.

Talk About It

Read each sentence. Is each underlined word a verb?

1. Maria <u>walks</u> to the park after school.
2. The boy <u>rides</u> his skateboard.
3. <u>Sharon</u> skips down the street.
4. A girl <u>pulls</u> a red wagon.
5. A <u>dog</u> chases a squirrel.

Skills Practice

If the underlined word is a verb, write **verb.** If the underlined word is not a verb, write **not verb.**

1. Ken <u>throws</u> the ball.
2. <u>Dora</u> swings the bat.
3. A girl <u>hits</u> the ball hard.
4. Jim <u>catches</u> the ball.
5. Jim throws the <u>ball</u> to Carlos.
6. Carlos <u>drops</u> the ball.
7. Dora <u>runs</u> to second base.

Writing Sentences

Think of a verb for each blank. Write each sentence.

1. My brother ____ his bicycle.
2. Rita ____ to the playground.
3. Mei ____ the football.
4. A cat ____ over the fence.

Sample Answer 1. verb

Verbs in Sentences

Verbs are important in sentences. You can find verbs in the predicate parts of sentences. Remember these two facts.

A **verb** is a word that names an action.

The **predicate part** of a sentence tells what action the subject part does.

- Look at the predicate part of each sentence. Read each verb.

Ben **walks** on the beach.

The man **runs** into the water.

Jan **dives.**

The woman **splashes** some water.

The main word in the predicate part of a sentence is the verb. The verb names the *action* that the subject part does.

- Read each sentence. Find the verb. What action does it name? The picture can help you.

My friends swim in a pool.
Ray splashes water on Sue.
Joe dives into the pool.
Maria floats on her back.

Talk About It

Read each sentence. Find the verb.

1. Our family drives to the lake every Sunday.
2. My cousins swim all day.
3. The babies build sand castles.
4. My mother puts a blanket on the sand.
5. Kim opens the picnic basket.
6. Her father swims in the deep water.

Skills Practice

Write each sentence. Underline the verb.

1. The class hikes in the woods.
2. The teacher carries a pack on his back.
3. The students pitch a tent.
4. Akiko builds a fire.
5. José cooks the food.
6. The teacher tells ghost stories.
7. Anna climbs into her sleeping bag.
8. An owl hoots.

Writing Sentences

Pretend you are having a picnic. Write four sentences to tell what you do on a picnic. Use these verbs.

1. run   3. eat
2. throw   4. sing

Sample Answer 1. The class hikes in the woods.

Verbs in the Present

A verb names an action. A verb can also tell *when* the action happens. Sometimes you talk about things that happen now.

- Look at these sentences that tell about the picture.

The girl <u>rides</u> a big horse.
The horses <u>jump</u> over the fence.

The sentences tell about things that happen now.
The verbs *rides* and *jump* are verbs in the present.

> A **verb in the present** names an action that happens now.

- Read each sentence.

John <u>walks</u> to the barn.   John <u>walked</u> to the barn.
Andy <u>cleans</u> the stall.   Andy <u>cleaned</u> the stall.
Paula <u>saddles</u> her horse.   Paula <u>saddled</u> her horse.

Look at the verbs in the sentences at the left. These verbs are verbs in the present. Look at the verbs in the sentences at the right. They are not in the present.

Talk About It

Find the verb in each sentence. Is the verb in the present?

1. Jane runs to the stable.
2. A little colt stands in a stall.
3. Jane hugs the colt.
4. The colt eats a piece of carrot.
5. The horses kicked their legs.
6. Jane talked to the colt.
7. The horses trot out of the stable.

Skills Practice

Read each sentence. Write **present** if the verb is in the present. Write **not present** if the verb is not in the present.

1. My sisters ride horses in the parade.
2. My dad tied ribbons on the horses.
3. Two other horses pull a wagon.
4. A family waits in the wagon.
5. Some children wave flags.
6. My mom waved to the children.
7. A man sells candy.
8. The band marches.
9. The band played my favorite song.
10. The crowd cheers loudly.
11. A police officer rides a horse.
12. The horse trots to the music.

Sample Answer 1. present

Using Verbs in the Present

You know that nouns are often in the subject parts of sentences. Remember that the *subject part* of a sentence names whom or what the sentence is about. Nouns in the subject part can be singular or plural.

A **singular noun** is a noun that names one person, place, or thing.

A **plural noun** is a noun that names more than one person, place, or thing.

- Read each sentence. Look at the noun in the subject part. Then look at the verb.

The boy runs.   Two boys run.

The sentences show that the verb must work with the noun in the subject part. The verb has different forms to work with singular and plural nouns.

- Read each pair of sentences. What is the ending on each verb? How does each verb change to work with the noun in the subject part?

Kurt *plays* with a ball.   The boys *play* marbles.
Kate *makes* candles.   Her sisters *make* paper airplanes.

Most verbs in the present end in *s* when they work with a *singular* noun. Most verbs in the present do not change at all when they work with a *plural* noun.

Talk About It

Read each sentence. Choose the verb that works
with the noun in the subject part.

1. Carmen ____ paper flowers.   (make, makes)
2. Her sisters ____ colored paper.   (buy, buys)
3. Sara ____ the paper into pieces.   (cut, cuts)
4. Paul ____ the pieces together.   (paste, pastes)
5. The boys ____ the edges.   (fold, folds)

Skills Practice

Write each sentence. Use the correct verb.

1. The boys ____ a lump of clay.   (find, finds)
2. Brian ____ a big piece.   (take, takes)
3. Fred ____ his clay.   (mold, molds)
4. The boy ____ a little house.   (build, builds)
5. Two girls ____ their clay.   (shape, shapes)
6. Their clay ____ into a vase.   (turn, turns)
7. Mother ____ more clay.   (buy, buys)

Writing Sentences

Pretend you and some friends are home on a rainy
day. You have crayons, paper, and scissors. You
are each going to make something.

1. Write one sentence to tell about what *one* friend
   makes.
2. Write one sentence to tell what *two* friends make
   together.

Sample Answer 1. The boys find a lump of clay.

Spelling Verbs

A verb in the present has different forms. You must know how to spell the form of the verb that you use in a sentence.

- Read each sentence.

The girl skate**s**.   Kim paint**s**.

The noun in each subject part is singular. The verb that works with each noun ends in -*s*.

> Add **-s** to most verbs in the present when they work with singular nouns.

Sometimes you add -*es* to a verb in the present when it works with a singular noun.

- Now read these sentences.

A player pass**es** the football.   Nancy watch**es** the game.

Notice the singular noun in each subject part. Each verb ends in -*es*.

> If a verb ends in **s, ss, ch, sh,** or **x,** add **-es** to make the verb work with a singular noun.

Sometimes you change the spelling of a verb before you add -*es*.

- Read each sentence. Notice that the spelling changes when this verb works with a singular noun.

The birds fly.   A bird flies.

If a verb ends with a **consonant** and **y**, change the **y** to **i** and add **-es** to make the correct form of the present.

Verbs in the present that work with *plural* nouns do not change.

- Read each sentence below.

Two boys sing a song.   The students listen.

Notice the nouns in the subject part. They are plural nouns. The verbs do not change.

Talk About It

What form of the verb belongs in each blank? Spell the verb.

1. Roberto ____ games.   (like)
2. A little boy ____ a kite.   (fly)
3. Tara ____ him.   (watch)

Skills Practice

Use a verb in the present in each blank. Write the sentence.

1. The students ____ hide-and-seek.   (play)
2. Liza ____ behind a tree.   (hide)
3. Gino ____ to find her.   (try)
4. The girl ____ out.   (peek)
5. The boy ____ her.   (catch)

Sample Answer **1.** The students play hide-and-seek.

Skills Review

If the underlined word is a verb, write **verb.** If the underlined word is not a verb, write **not verb.**

1. Molly <u>finds</u> a pretty leaf.
2. Rita <u>traces</u> it on paper.
3. The girl writes with a <u>pencil</u>.
4. A <u>boy</u> colors it.
5. Peter <u>cuts</u> it out.
6. The teacher <u>pins</u> it to the board.

Read each sentence. Write the verb.

7. The boys make a book cover.
8. Jerry buys some brown paper.
9. Pablo cuts a piece of it.
10. Ben folds the piece in half.
11. Carl puts the book on it.
12. The girls bend the edges around the book.

Read each sentence. Write **present** if the verb is in the present. Write **not present** if the verb is not in the present.

13. Matt finds a shell at the beach.
14. The shell sparkled in the sun.
15. Carol makes a necklace.
16. Her father cleaned the shell.
17. Her mother drilled a hole in it.
18. Carol puts a ribbon through the hole.
19. Carol likes the necklace.

Read each sentence. Write the correct verb.

20. Anna ____ a garden.   (plant, plants)
21. Her father ____ some holes.   (dig, digs)
22. Mike ____ the seeds.   (buy, buys)
23. The girls ____ the garden.   (water, waters)
24. The seeds ____ .   (grow, grows)

Use a verb in the present in each blank. Write the verb.

25. Judy ____ in the shade.   (sit)
26. Her sister ____ the ducks in the pond.   (watch)
27. Judy ____ a swan.   (see)
28. The boys ____ around.   (run)
29. Ducks ____ fish.   (like)
30. The bird ____ away.   (fly)
31. My father ____ the children.   (call)
32. A dog ____ the pond.   (pass)

Play this verb game. Have one person write five different verbs (such as *dance, hop, throw*) on five pieces of paper. Fold the papers and put them in a hat.

Someone chooses a paper and acts out the verb. The class tries to name the action being done. The person who guesses the answer must spell the verb. He or she then becomes the next person to act out a verb.

Exploring Language

Verbs in the Past

Some verbs name actions that happen now. Other verbs name actions that happened before.

The boy climbs a tree.   The boy climbed a tree.

- Look at the sentence under each picture. The sentence on the left tells about something that happens *now*. The sentence on the right tells about something that happened *before*. *Climbed* is a verb in the past.

> A **verb in the past** names an action that happened before.

- Read each sentence. What is the verb? Is the verb in the past?

Adam <u>played</u> in the treehouse.   Jean <u>opened</u> the door.
A girl <u>knocked.</u>   Lucy <u>chases</u> a squirrel.

Look at the underlined words. They are verbs. The first three verbs are in the past. They tell what happened before. The last verb is in the present.

Talk About It

Find the verb in each sentence. Is the verb in the past?

1. The children played with model trains.
2. The train moves on the track.
3. Ann pulled the engine.
4. The train crossed the bridge.
5. Jack pushed the train.
6. The children listen to the whistle.

Skills Practice

Read each sentence. Write **past** if the verb is in the past. Write **not past** if the verb is not in the past.

1. Mandy raced home.
2. The girl called her brother.
3. Jim plays games.
4. Mandy played cards.
5. Her brother opened a drawer.
6. Jim hands a deck of cards to Mandy.
7. Mandy counted the cards.
8. Mandy changes the score.
9. The children played all afternoon.
10. The children like the game.
11. Mandy wins very often.
12. Jim added the scores.
13. The boy continued the game.
14. Their mother called them.
15. The children started their homework.

Sample Answer 1. past

Spelling Verbs in the Past

Sometimes you talk about something that happened before. You use a verb in the past. Most verbs in the past have the same ending.

Add **-ed** to most verbs to make a verb in the past.

If a verb ends with **e**, drop the **e** and add **-ed** to make the correct form of the past.

• Read each sentence. Look at the verb.

The family camped in the forest.   Ed cooked.
Paula moved the tent.   A wolf howled.

The verbs are in the past. Each verb ends in *-ed*.

Sometimes you have to change the spelling of a verb before you add *-ed*.

• Look at each pair of verbs.

| tr y | carr y | cop y |
| tr ied | carr ied | cop ied |

You can see that the spelling changes for each verb in the past.

If a verb ends with a **consonant** and **y,** change the **y** to **i** and add **-ed** to make a verb in the past.

Talk About It

Find the verb in each sentence. Is it about the past or the present? How can you tell?

1. The friends hiked for a long time.
2. Inés finds a good place for a camp.
3. Debra fished in the lake.
4. Barry fried fish over the fire.

Skills Practice

Write each sentence. Use the verb in the past.
1. Amy ___ the trail last week.   (mark)
2. The boys ___ the packs then.   (carry)
3. Ed ___ many interesting leaves yesterday.   (pick)
4. The girls ___ the dishes after lunch.   (dry)
5. Larry ___ the dishes to the tent.   (move)
6. Ed ___ the new flashlight.   (try)
7. The family ___ the dinner last night.   (like)
8. The friends ___ the trip last week.   (enjoy)

Writing Sentences

Pretend you slept in a tent in the woods last night. Write two sentences about something that happened.

Sample Answer 1. Amy marked the trail last week.

Verb Synonyms

You and your friends do not always use the same words to tell about the same thing. Sometimes you use different verbs to tell about the same thing in different ways.

- Read each sentence about the picture.

The children *walked.*   The children *hiked.*
The children *marched.*   The children *strolled.*

The sentences tell about the same thing. The verbs *walked, marched, hiked,* and *strolled* all mean almost the same thing. But the verb *marched* most closely names the action in the picture.

You can write better sentences if you choose verbs carefully. The verb you choose can change the meaning of a sentence.

- Read each sentence. How does each verb change the sentence?

The boy ___ the package. (carried, hauled)
A girl ___ to school. (ran, raced)

Talk About It

Read each sentence about the picture. Which verb most closely names the action in the picture?

1. The horse ____ in the park.
   (walks, trots)
2. Linda ____ the reins.
   (holds, has)
3. The horse ____ the wagon.
   (pulls, moves)
4. Steve and Linda ____ in the wagon.
   (roll, ride)

Skills Practice

Read each sentence about the picture. Choose the verb that most closely names the action in the picture. Write the sentence.

1. Ray ____ an apron.
   (wears, uses)
2. Ray ____ a bowl.
   (grabs, takes)
3. Ray ____ a cup of flour.
   (adds, dumps)
4. Ray ____ the spoon.
   (has, holds)
5. Ray ____ the dough.
   (mixes, stirs)
6. Ray ____ the bread.
   (cooks, bakes)

Sample Answer 1. Ray wears an apron.

Skills Review

Read each sentence. Write **past** if the verb is in the past. Write **not past** if the verb is not in the past.

1. Linda walks in the woods.
2. Robin picked some flowers.
3. Betty walked with her friends.
4. A deer jumped over a log.
5. The girls play under a tree.
6. Mark dried the twigs.
7. Linda feeds a squirrel.
8. The girl carried the rock.
9. The children chased a butterfly.
10. Linda searched for a bird's nest.

Read each sentence. Write the verb in the past.

11. Diana ___ baseball. (play)
12. The girl ___ the ball to Jack. (toss)
13. The boy ___ on first base. (jump)
14. Our mother ___ the children. (call)
15. My grandmother ___ dinner. (cook)
16. Jack ___ Diana home. (follow)
17. Bill ___ his dog yesterday. (walk)
18. The dog ___ a cat. (chase)
19. The cat ___ a tree. (climb)
20. The dog ___ a new dog food. (try)
21. Bill ___ to his dog. (wave)
22. Bill ___ home. (hurry)

Read each sentence about the picture. Choose the verb that most closely names the action in the picture. Write the verb.

23. Dennis ____ on the ground.
    (moved, crawled)
24. The boy ____ a bird's nest.
    (saw, studied)
25. Marie ____ a heavy basket.
    (dragged, carried)
26. The girl ____ hello to Dennis.
    (said, shouted)
27. A duck ____ to the lake.
    (waddled, walked)

Look at the sentence.

I *walked* to school.

Try to think of other verbs you can use instead of *walked* that mean almost the same thing. Go around the room and ask each person in your class to put a different verb in the sentence. Those who cannot think of one must drop out. The winner is the last person left who knows another word for *walked*.

Exploring Language

Following and Giving Directions

Sometimes you have to tell someone how to do something. *Directions* tell you how to do things. You must follow directions carefully to do things in the right way.

Ben's teacher gave the class two directions. First she asked them to draw a picture of what they like best in the park. Next she asked them to write a sentence about their pictures.

- Look at the children's papers.

Lee followed directions. His picture shows what he likes best in the park. His sentence tells what he likes best in the park. Rob's picture shows something in the park. But he did not write a sentence. Cindy's picture just shows something she likes. It is not about the park.

Directions can tell how to get somewhere. Good directions make sense. They help people to find places easily. Be sure you tell things in the right order when you give directions.

Maps can help you give directions.

● Find Lee's house on the map. Follow these directions to get to the park from Lee's house.

First walk up Pine Road to School Street.
Next turn left at School Street.
Last walk to the park.

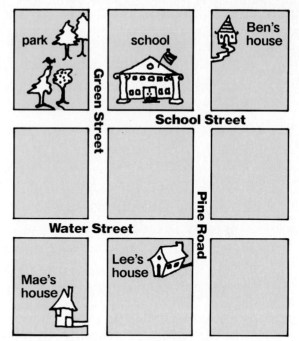

Talk About It

Use the map above. Give directions to get from Mae's house to school. Use words like *first, next,* and *last* in your directions.

Skills Practice

Mae gave directions to get from her house to Ben's house. Her directions are not in the right order. Write them in the correct order. Use the map above to help you. Use words like *first, next,* and *last* when you write the directions in order.

Turn right at Water Street and walk to Pine Road.
Walk up Green Street to Water Street.
Turn left at Pine Road and walk up to Ben's house.

Using Test Taking Skills

You take many tests in school. Tests can help you find out what you know. They can also help you find out what you need to study some more. You can help yourself do better on tests if you follow a few rules.

1. **Get Ready.** Be sure that you have pens, pencils, and paper for taking the test.
2. **Follow Directions.** Listen carefully if your teacher reads the directions to you. Read the directions carefully if you read them to yourself.
   Be sure to ask any questions before you begin.
3. **Mark your answers.** Be sure you mark your answers in the correct place. Often you write your answers beside the questions on your test paper. Sometimes you write your answer under the questions. Other times you use a separate answer sheet.

- Look at the test below. In this example, answers are marked in a special place on the test paper.

Choose the right word to complete each sentence. Fill in the circle for the right answer. Write only in the answer row.	Name _Sue Jones_ Date _May 8, 1981_ Grade _3-C_ Answer Row
1. The plural of train is ____. **A.** traine **B.** trains **C.** train	1.　　A　　B　　C　　○　　●　　○
2. The plural of bus is ____. **A.** busse **B.** buss **C.** buses	2.　　A　　B　　C　　○　　○　　●

Talk About It

Look again at the test paper.

1. Find where you would write your name.
2. What two things would you write below your name?
3. How would you mark the right answer to the first question? The second?

Skills Practice

Read the following test paper. Look carefully at how the person has followed directions. Write the answers to the questions below on your own paper.

Choose the right word to complete each sentence. Fill in the circle for the right answer. Write only in the answer row.	Name _Luis Vargas_ Date _3-A_ Grade _March 6, 1981_ Answer Row
1. The girls _find_ pretty rocks. **A.** finds **B.** find	**1.** A B O O
2. Father ____ a long walk. **A.** takes **B.** take	**2.** Ⓐ B O O
3. The boys _play_ a new game. **A.** play **B.** plays	**3.** A B ● O

1. What is wrong with the date and the grade?
2. How should the right answer to the first question be marked?
3. What is wrong with how the answer to the second question is marked?
4. What is wrong with how the answer to the third question is marked?

Direction Paragraphs

Thinking About Paragraphs

Directions are important. They tell people the things they need to know. Directions must always be clear. Then people understand what to do.

At times you may have to give directions aloud. Sometimes you write directions in a paragraph. The paragraph has a main idea sentence and several detail sentences. The main idea sentence tells what the directions are for. The detail sentences tell how to do or make something. Each detail sentence gives one step of the directions. The sentences must come in an order that makes sense. They should tell what to do <u>first</u>, <u>second</u>, and <u>third</u>.

- Read this paragraph that gives directions.

It is fun to make a fruit basket. First you find a large basket. Second you put in an apple, a pear, and an orange. Third you tie a ribbon around the basket.

Talking About Paragraphs

1. What is the main idea sentence in the paragraph?
2. Which sentences give the steps for making a fruit basket?
3. What words are used to show the order of the steps?

A Class Paragraph

Your class is going to write a direction paragraph together. Look at the map. Find Todd's house. Find the library. Write directions that explain how to get from Todd's house to the library. Your teacher will write your direction paragraph on the board.

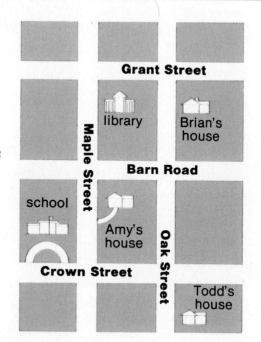

1. Start your paragraph with this main idea sentence: *Follow these directions to go to the library from Todd's house.*

2. Think of a detail sentence that tells how to get from Oak Street to Barn Road. You might write: *Walk up Oak Street to Barn Road.*

3. Think of a detail sentence that tells how to get from Barn Road to Maple Street. Will you turn left or right?

4. Think of a detail sentence that tells how to get from Maple Street to the library. Will you turn left or right?

5. Read your paragraph. Are the directions written in clear, step-by-step order?

6. Write the paragraph on your paper. Remember to indent the first word.

Practicing a Direction Paragraph

Thinking About Your Paragraph

You are going to write a direction paragraph about how to make a bean bag. You may also choose your own topic.

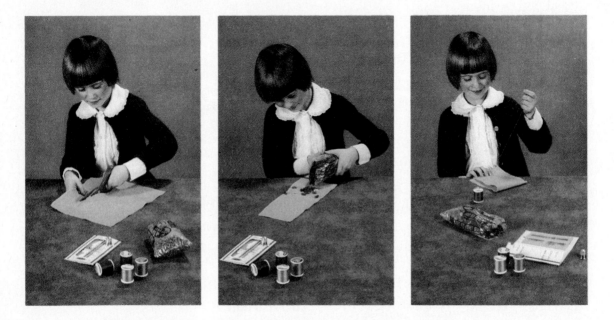

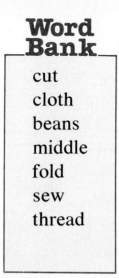

Word Bank

cut
cloth
beans
middle
fold
sew
thread

Writing Your Paragraph

1. Start your paragraph with this main idea sentence: A bean bag is fun to make.
2. Look at the pictures. Write detail sentences that give directions for making a bean bag. You will have three detail sentences.
3. Use the Word Bank to help you spell the words. You may want to use the words <u>first</u>, <u>second</u>, and <u>third</u> to write your directions clearly

Edit Your Paragraph

Read your finished paragraph. Think about these questions as you read.

1. Are your directions clear and in correct order?
2. What verbs did you use in your detail sentences? Does each sentence have a verb that tells what to do?
3. Are capital letters and period used correctly? Did you indent the first word?
4. Did you spell all words correctly? Correct your mistakes. If you need to, write your paragraph again.

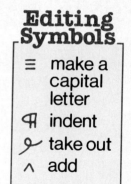

Editing Symbols

≡ make a capital letter
¶ indent
✄ take out
∧ add

INDEPENDENT WRITING
A Direction Paragraph

Prewriting Writing clear directions takes practice. Suppose a new student has come to your class. You have been asked to write directions that will tell the student how to get from your classroom to the lunchroom. Draw a simple map. Then jot down notes that tell the student where to go.

Writing Now write a direction paragraph that tells a new student how to get from your classroom to the lunchroom. Start your paragraph with a main idea sentence. Then look at your notes. Make sure they are in the right order. Now you may want to add your map to your directions.

Editing Use the check questions and the editing symbols above to edit your direction paragraph.

Invitations

Thinking About Invitations

Pretend you are planning a party. Notes must be sent to the people you want to invite. These notes are called *invitations*. An invitation tells people what they need to know about the party.

- Look at the invitation below.

Please come to my birthday party.
Name: Kay Johnson
Place: 88 Bell Road
Date: Friday, May 10
Time: 4:00
Telephone: 588-9842

Talking About Invitations

Read the invitation above.
1. Who is giving the party?
2. Where and when is the party being held?
3. What telephone number can people call to say if they are coming?

Writing an Invitation

Write your own invitation. Copy the part of the above invitation that is in dark print. Then write your own name. Write the place, date, and time of the party. Give your telephone number so people can call you.

Telephone Messages

Thinking About Telephone Messages

Sometimes you take directions instead of giving them. For example, you might answer a telephone call that is for someone else. You need to take a message that tells about the call.

- Look at the telephone message below.

A call for: Jill
Caller's name: David Murphy
Time: 1:00
Message: David is coming to your party.
Caller's number: 566-3209
Message taken by: Burt

Talking About Telephone Messages

1. Who was the above message for? Who called?
2. What time was the call? What was the message?
3. What is the caller's number? Who took the message?

Writing a Telephone Message

Pretend you have a brother named Jim who is planning a birthday party. At 4:30 Martha Keller calls Jim to say she cannot come to the party. Martha's phone number is 533-5892. Copy the part of the above message that is in dark print. Then fill in the information.

Unit Review

If the underlined word is a verb, write **verb.** If the underlined word is not a verb, write **not verb.** *pages 70-71*

1. Mario <u>walks</u> in the rain.
2. <u>Diane</u> steps in a puddle.
3. The girl <u>wears</u> boots.
4. A boy carries a <u>coat</u>.

Read each sentence. Write the verb. *pages 72-73*

5. Jim builds a snow fort.
6. The boys skate here.
7. Judy throws a snowball.
8. Carol rides her sled.

Read each sentence. Write **present** if the verb is in the present. Write **not present** if the verb is not in the present. *pages 74-75*

9. Cindy enjoys the breeze.
10. A baby laughed happily.
11. The boy wears a sweater.
12. Dave jumps down.

Read each sentence. Write the correct verb. *pages 76-77*

13. The boy ___ a big kite. (make, makes)
14. The wind ___ hard. (blow, blows)
15. The kite ___ on the breeze. (sail, sails)
16. Our friends ___ the kite. (follow, follows)

Use a verb in the present in each blank. Write the verb. *pages 78-79*

17. Karen ___ a piece of paper. (fold)
18. Her little brother ___ her. (watch)
19. The boy ___ the paper airplane. (fly)
20. Some girls ___ more toys. (make)

Read each sentence. Write **past** if the verb is in the past. Write **not past** if the verb is not in the past. *pages 82-83*

21. The children played hockey.
22. Joe skated very fast.
23. Maria hits the puck.
24. Their team scored a goal.

Read each sentence. Write the verb in the past. *pages 84-85*

25. Stan ___ the eggs.   (cook)
26. The girls ___ the bread.   (butter)
27. Ruth ___ the potatoes.   (fry)
28. The family ___ the breakfast.   (like)

Now you will write an invitation.

29. Here is the information you include in an invitation. Write it on your paper. *page 98*

Name: _____

Place: _____

Date: _____

Time: _____

Telephone: _____

Pretend that John Williams is planning his birthday party. It is to be held at 25 Oak Lane on June 24. The party will start at 2:00. John's phone number is 589-5332. Write the invitation that John will send to his friends.

A Story in Pictures

Most stories are told in words. Some stories can be told without using any words. A story can be told in pictures. Each picture tells part of the story. You must study each picture to understand what happens in the story.

Look at each picture in this story.

CREATIVE EXPRESSION: *Non-verbal Communication*

CREATIVE EXPRESSION: *Non-verbal Communication*

Creative Activities

1. Creative Writing The children in *The Surprise* made a *piñata*. Do you think they were surprised by what was hidden inside? Write a paragraph that tells how to make a *piñata*. Use the pictures to help you.

2. Pretend you are one of these people. Act out what the person is doing. Do not speak. Ask the class to guess what you are doing.

A person climbing many stairs
A batter hitting a ball
A person flying a kite
A lion tamer with a lion

3. Make pictures of your own. Think about what you want in each picture. How will your story begin and end? How many pictures will your story have? Share your picture story with someone.

TELEPHONE REPAIRMEN

Grammar and Related Language Skills

Review of Sentences
Nouns and Verbs in Sentences
Pronouns in Sentences
Possessive Pronouns
Punctuating a Conversation

Practical Communication

STUDY AND REFERENCE SKILLS
Using a Dictionary

COMPOSITION
Writing a Thank-You Note

Creative Expression

A Play

What kind of job would you like to have someday?
People must apply for the jobs they want. Sometimes they send a letter with information about
their past experiences. Sometimes people present
themselves in an interview. How would good writing
and speaking skills help a person apply for a job
or do a job well?

Reviewing Kinds of Sentences

You have learned about three kinds of sentences.

A **telling sentence** is a sentence that tells something.

A **question sentence** is a sentence that asks something.

An **exclamation sentence** is a sentence that shows strong feeling.

- Read each sentence. Is it a telling sentence, a question sentence, or an exclamation sentence?

What a funny puppet show we saw!
Did you ever see a talking potato?
A boy put a potato on a stick.
He painted a face on the potato.
How funny the jokes were!
Do you like puppet shows?

You use special signs when you write sentences. One special sign shows where each sentence begins. You use other special signs to show where a sentence ends.

Use a **capital letter** to begin the first word of every sentence.

Use a **period** (.) at the end of a telling sentence.

Use a **question mark** (**?**) at the end of a question sentence.

Use an **exclamation mark** (**!**) at the end of an exclamation sentence.

Talk About It

Read each sentence. Look at the beginning and end of each sentence. What special signs are missing?

1. The class saw a puppet
2. Who moved the puppet
3. How hard we laughed

4. a puppet told a story.
5. can puppets really talk
6. Can we make puppets

Skills Practice

Write each sentence correctly. Then write **telling** if it is a telling sentence. Write **question** if it is a question sentence. Write **exclamation** if it is an exclamation sentence.

1. Juan likes to sing
2. he listens to the radio.
3. did you hear a new song
4. do you like music?

5. can you play the piano?
6. how well Karen plays!
7. she likes to sing, too.
8. what a pretty song that is!

Sample Answer 1. Juan likes to sing. Telling

Complete Sentences

You have learned that a sentence is a group of words that states a complete idea. Every sentence has a subject part and a predicate part.

The **subject part** of a sentence names whom or what the sentence is about.

The **predicate part** of a sentence tells what action the subject part does.

Each part alone is not a sentence. The two parts work together to state a complete idea.

SUBJECT PART	PREDICATE PART
The cook	made blueberry pancakes.

- Read each group of words. Which groups of words are sentences?

The baker makes bread.   Eats the bread.
The baker.   Barbara eats the bread.

- Read each sentence. Find the subject part. Find the predicate part.

A scientist found some old bones.
People put the bones together.
The people make a dinosaur.

Talk About It

Read each group of words. Is it a complete sentence? What do you need to add to make a complete sentence?

1. A ball player.
2. The team wins a game.
3. Hits a home run.
4. Sells orange juice.
5. The team.
6. The crowd yells.

Skills Practice

Write each sentence. Draw a line between the subject part and the predicate part.

1. A train moves fast.
2. The man buys a ticket.
3. People go many places.
4. The bell rang.
5. The class stands up.
6. A girl opens the door.

Add a subject part or a predicate part to complete each sentence.

7. The teacher ____ .
8. My doctor ____ .
9. A bus driver ____ .
10. ____ sells shoes.
11. ____ draws pictures.
12. ____ throws a ball.

Writing Sentences

Pretend you are a TV star. Write a telling sentence about being a TV star. Be sure your sentence has a subject part and a predicate part.

Sample Answer 1. A train | moves fast.

Nouns and Verbs in Sentences

You know that words like *Chris, street,* and *apple* name people, places, or things.

A **noun** is a word that names a person, a place, or a thing.

Most sentences have a noun in the subject part. Some sentences have a noun in the predicate part.

- Read each sentence. Find the noun in the subject part. Is there a noun in the predicate part?

The show starts.　　　　　The crowd likes the show.
A dancer jumps in the air.　The dancer bows.

You know that words like *run* and *jump* name actions.

A **verb** is a word that names an action.

Every sentence has a verb in the predicate part.

- Read each sentence. Find the verb.

Patty brought some wood.　Snappy likes the doghouse.
Len painted the doghouse.　Snappy sleeps on the roof.

Remember that the verb must work with the noun in the subject part.

- Read each pair of sentences. How does the verb change to work with the noun in the subject part?

The teacher <u>helps</u>.　　One cook <u>makes</u> lunch.
The teachers <u>help</u>.　　Two cooks <u>make</u> soup.

Talk About It

Read these sentences. Find the nouns and verbs.

1. The builders make houses.
2. The workers build a roof.
3. A man paints the walls.
4. The boy opens a window.
5. A woman fixes the doors.
6. A girl hangs pictures.

Skills Practice

Write each sentence. Draw one line under each noun. Draw two lines under each verb.

1. A girl plants seeds.
2. The little plants grow.
3. Plants grow in the sun.
4. Horses eat hay.
5. The flowers bloom.
6. A girl works on a ranch.
7. The man rides a horse.
8. The horses live in a barn.
9. A girl waters the plants.
10. A horse trots.

Write the correct verb for each sentence.

11. My friend ____ on a farm. (live, lives)
12. The chickens ____ corn. (eat, eats)
13. A goat ____ the flowers. (like, likes)
14. The farmers ____ very hard. (work, works)
15. The pigs ____ in the pen. (sit, sits)
16. A horse ____ in the field. (run, runs)

Writing Sentences

Pretend that you drive a bus. Write two sentences about two different things you might do on your job. What nouns and verbs did you use?

Sample Answers 1. A girl plants seeds. 11. lives

Skills Review

Write each sentence correctly. Then write **telling** if it is a telling sentence. Write **question** if it is a question sentence. Write **exclamation** if it is an exclamation sentence.

1. how badly my arm hurts!
2. did you fall?
3. you should go to the doctor
4. What happens there
5. the doctor looks at your arm.
6. what a big machine he uses!
7. the doctor can see you now.

Read each sentence. Write the subject part.

8. The pilot flies a big airplane.
9. The airplane travels very fast.
10. An airplane flew to Detroit.
11. Many people ride on airplanes.
12. Animals fly on airplanes.

Read each sentence. Write the predicate part.

13. People eat on airplanes.
14. Airplanes fly over the ocean.
15. My suitcase fell off the plane.
16. A man found the suitcase.
17. A woman gave the suitcase to me.

Read each sentence. Write the nouns.

18. The woman plows the field.
19. Andy plants corn.
20. The farmers feed the chickens.
21. The chickens eat.
22. The chickens gobble the corn.

Read each sentence. Write the verbs.

23. Robin sews shirts.
24. Joy works in a store.
25. The store buys the shirts.
26. Many people look at the shirts.
27. Joy sells the new clothes.

Write the correct verb for each sentence.

28. A child ___ a book. (read, reads)
29. A man ___ the house. (clean, cleans)
30. The dancers ___ pretty clothes. (wear, wears)
31. The cooks ___ soup. (make, makes)
32. The woman ___ . (write, writes)

house   book   SINGER

Find three nouns in a newspaper.
Cut them out. Draw a picture to
show what each noun names.

Exploring Language

Pronouns in Sentences

Many sentences have nouns in the subject part. Sometimes you can use other words in place of these nouns.

A **pronoun** is a word that takes the place of one or more nouns.

These are the pronouns that can be used in the subject part of a sentence.

I	you	she he it
we		they

Remember to use a capital letter for the pronoun *I*.

- Read each pair of sentences. What pronoun is in the subject part of the second sentence in each pair? What noun does each pronoun replace?

Rita makes a basket.
She makes a basket.

The girls make kites.
They make kites.

Eddie paints two bowls.
He paints two bowls.

The market opens early.
It opens early.

- Read these sentences. What is the pronoun in each sentence?

I paint the room.
You fix the chair.
We work hard all day.

Talk About It

Read each pair of sentences. Write the second sentence using the correct pronoun.

1. Ben works in the city.
____ sells cars.

2. Jenny works in the city.
____ writes books.

3. Jenny and Ben ride.
____ ride a train.

4. The train leaves early.
____ is crowded.

Skills Practice

Write each sentence. Underline each pronoun.

1. I shoveled snow.
2. You helped.

3. We earned a dollar.
4. They watched.

Read each pair of sentences. Write the second sentence using the correct pronoun.

5. Mrs. Lee drives a bus.
____ drives carefully.

6. The bus goes to school.
____ is full of children.

7. Ed rides the bus.
____ sits quietly.

8. Ed and Jane sit together.
____ sing together.

9. Mr. Harris is a teacher.
____ teaches third grade.

10. The bell rings.
____ rings again.

11. Jane raises her hand.
____ answers the question.

12. Jane and Ed carry books.
____ have homework today.

Sample Answers 1. I shoveled snow. **5.** She drives carefully.

Using Pronouns and Verbs

The subject part of every sentence has a noun or a pronoun. The predicate part has a verb. You know that nouns and verbs must work together in a sentence. Pronouns and verbs must also work together in a sentence.

- Read each sentence. Name each pronoun. What ending is used on each verb?

He teach**es** ice skating.
She pick**s** fruit.
It fall**s** off trees.

- Read these sentences. What pronouns are used? Verbs used with these pronouns do not have *s* or *es* endings.

You skate very well.
They pack the fruit in boxes.
We like the fruit.
I eat fruit before skating.

- Read each sentence. Find the pronoun and verb. Do they work together in each sentence?

I enjoy ice skating.
She enjoys skating.
We skate together every week.
He skates very fast.

Talk About It

Use the correct verb in each sentence.

1. He ___ a truck every day.   (drive, drives)
2. I ___ my homework quickly.   (finish, finishes)
3. They ___ cars.   (fix, fixes)
4. She ___ in a post office.   (work, works)

Skills Practice

Use the correct verb in each sentence. Write the verb.

1. We ___ in the snow.   (play, plays)
2. I ___ the snow fall.   (watch, watches)
3. They ___ the schools.   (close, closes)
4. We ___ home when it snows.   (stay, stays)
5. They ___ the roads in the afternoon.   (plow, plows)
6. You ___ cold quickly.   (get, gets)
7. He ___ the walk.   (shovel, shovels)
8. She ___ a heavy coat all winter.   (wear, wears)
9. It ___ her warm.   (keep, keeps)
10. We ___ to school today.   (return, returns)

Writing Sentences

Pretend you work in a pet store. Write a sentence using each pronoun. Be sure to use the correct verb.

1. I   2. it   3. they   4. we

Sample Answer 1. play

Possessive Pronouns

You know that a pronoun is a word that takes the place of one or more nouns. *Possessive pronouns* show who or what has or owns something.

> A **possessive pronoun** is a pronoun that shows who or what has or owns something.

- Suppose your name were Tom. You want to talk about your brother. If you could not use possessive pronouns, you would have to say:

Tom's brother works in a store.

- Now read this sentence.

My brother works in a store.

This time, the possessive pronoun *my* is used in place of the possessive noun *Tom's*.

- Look at the box. The possessive pronouns on the left are used in sentences on the right.

my	My mother owns a store.
her	Her store is in town.
your	Your father is a doctor.
his	His office has blue walls.
its	Its rooms are big.
our	Our parents are busy.
their	Their jobs are interesting.

Talk About It

Read each pair of sentences. Choose the possessive pronoun that belongs in each blank space.

1. Steve is a farmer.
___ farm has many cows.   (His, Her)

2. Laura works for Steve.
___ job is to feed the animals.   (His, Her)

3. The horses are hungry.
___ food is in the barn.   (Our, Their)

Skills Practice

Read each pair of sentences. Write the second sentence. Use the correct pronoun.

1. I work in a library.
___ job is to put away the books.   (Their, My)

2. You live in Greenville.
___ town has a bigger library.   (Your, His)

3. Greenville is a city.
___ streets are busy.   (Its, Our)

4. My family lives in Ohio.
___ town is quiet.   (Its, Our)

5. I have a dog.
___ dog does tricks.   (Your, My)

6. Jorge has a cat.
___ cat sleeps all day.   (His, Her)

Sample Answer 1. My job is to put away the books.

Punctuating a Conversation

When you talk with someone else, you have a conversation. In a conversation, you say things to another person. The words that are spoken are called a *conversation*.

Sometimes you write a conversation. Then you use a special way of writing. You follow certain rules:

Put **quotation marks** (" ") around the words that each person says.

Joey said, " My uncle is a builder. He built the green house across the street. "

Use a **conversation word** such as *said, whispered,* or *called* to tell how the person talked.

Use a **comma** (,) after the conversation word.

Gail answered , "My aunt also builds houses. She built the house she lives in."

Put a **period** (.) before the last quotation mark at the end of the sentence.

Joey added, "Next month my uncle will help put up the new library."

Indent the first word each time a new person talks.

Capitalize the first word in each quotation.

→Gail stated, " My aunt plans to work on the library, too."

Talk About It

Read each sentence. Tell where punctuation and capital letters belong.

1. Jane said I would like these books.
2. The librarian stated you may borrow them for two weeks
3. Jane replied I may need them longer
4. The librarian said call us if you need to keep them longer.
5. Jane answered thank you very much

Skills Practice

Write each sentence. Add punctuation and capital letters where they belong.

1. Lucy said my aunt takes care of animals.
2. Paul stated I take care of our cat
3. Lucy replied Aunt Sue is an animal doctor
4. Paul said she must see many kinds of animals.
5. Lucy answered She works at the zoo
6. Paul declared the zoo sure has many animals.
7. Lucy said Aunt Sue just treated an elephant.
8. Paul exclaimed an elephant is a big patient
9. Lucy replied it just had a sore toe.
10. Paul added I hope it feels better now

Sample Answer 1. Lucy said, "My aunt takes care of animals."

Skills Review

Read each sentence. Write each pronoun.

1. I cleaned the room.
2. She washed the windows.
3. They looked very dirty.
4. He dusted the table.

5. It needed a tablecloth.
6. We worked hard.
7. You can finish the job.
8. Then we will rest.

Read each pair of sentences. Write the correct
pronoun for the second sentence.

9. Ann made a pot.
   ____ used clay.

10. Dan painted the pot.
    ____ used red paint.

11. The pot looked empty.
    ____ needed something.

12. Joe and Dan had two seeds.
    ____ put seeds in the pot.

Use the correct verb in each sentence. Write the verb.

13. She ____ music.   (teach, teaches)
14. He ____ the drums.   (play, plays)
15. You ____ the piano.   (play, plays)
16. We ____ the band today at noon. (join, joins)
17. They ____ our music.   (like, likes)

Read each pair of sentences. Write the second
sentence using the correct pronoun.

18. Mr. Ramos works hard.
    ____ job is important.   (Our, His)

19. Ms. Ria goes to the bank.
    ____ money is there.   (Her, Their)

20. We have a bank, too.

_____ bank is small.   (Our, Its)

21. Ms. Ames bakes.

_____ bread is hot.   (Her, Your)

22. Bakers sell rolls, too.

_____ rolls sell quickly.   (Our, Their)

23. That cake looks good.

_____ frosting is pink.   (Our, Its)

Write each sentence. Add punctuation and capital letters where they belong.

24. Ted said Mr. Lin drives a taxicab

25. Cindy answered he must drive very well

26. Ted added He also knows our city well

27. Cindy said mr. Lin has many street maps.

28. Ted declared he can find new places fast.

29. Cindy stated I'll drive a taxicab someday

BUS STOP

There are many words that sound the same. But they do not mean the same thing. Look at these words.

Our bus comes in an hour.
We saw a tiny, wee flower.
I have something in my eye.

Can you think of others?

Exploring Language

Using a Dictionary

The words in a dictionary are in alphabetical order. This means that the words come in the same order as the letters of the alphabet.

You may want to know if a list of words is in alphabetical order. Look at the first letter of each word. The letters should come in the same order as the letters of the alphabet. Many words begin with the same letter. Then you must look at the second letter. These two lists are in alphabetical order.

detective welcome
helicopter whale
trail   worker

Suppose the first and second letters of each word are the same. Then you must look at the third letter to see if the words are in alphabetical order.

- Look at the three words in each list. Are they in alphabetical order?

beginning grant mirror
bean   grin   mistake
below   grocery mix

You can find words in a dictionary more quickly if you know which part to turn to. Think of dividing the dictionary into two parts. All words beginning with *a* through *m* are in the first part. All words beginning with *n* through *z* are in the second part.

• Read each word. Would you find it in the first part or the second part of a dictionary?

vegetable   company   practice   horn

Talk About It

Put each list of three words in alphabetical order.

1. drop	**2.** themselves	**3.** beach	**4.** state
written	ticket	bend	storm
march	television	bee	steam

Skills Practice

Write each list of three words in alphabetical order.

1. frog	**2.** open	**3.** teacher	**4.** problem
could	many	talk	prepare
train	minute	thin	print

Read each word at the left. Does it come between the words in **a** or in **b**? Write the letter of the correct pair of words.

5. lesson   **a.** lend, let   **6.** friend   **a.** four, frame
          b. letter, life   **b.** fresh, frog

Would you find each word in the first part or the second part of a dictionary? Write your answer.

7. language   **8.** polite   **9.** sky   **10.** edge

Sample Answers **1.** could frog train **5.** a **7.** first part

Alphabetical Order in a Dictionary

Sometimes you need to look up words in a dictionary. You can find words quickly if you know how to use a dictionary. The words in a dictionary are put in alphabetical order. *Alphabetical order* means that words are placed in the same order as the letters of the alphabet.

A B C D E F G H I J K L M N O P Q R S T U V W X Y Z

- Look at the three words in each list. All the words have the same first letter. But they have different second letters. Look at the alphabet. Are these words in alphabetical order?

ladder	smell	game
leak	scare	glass
lizard	see	give

- Look at the three words in each list. The first two letters of each word are the same. But the third letter of each word is different. Look at the alphabet. Are these words in alphabetical order?

molasses	flutter	cream
money	fleece	cross
mouth	flower	crazy

Talk About It

Put the words in each list in alphabetical order.

1. thirsty
trudge
tan

2. careless
close
candle

3. peak
perform
peck

Skills Practice

Write the words in each list in alphabetical order.

1. skirt
shock
simply

5. beef
banker
boss

9. wool
wobble
worker

2. message
meal
medal

6. prize
sound
puppet

10. relay
rejoice
regular

3. away
art
arm

7. rosy
rough
roam

11. egg
eight
else

4. silver
belong
hour

8. slide
iron
jet

12. noise
next
number

Sample Answer **1.** shock simply skirt

Introductions

Thinking About Introductions

What happens when a new person comes to your class? Your teacher may tell you the person's name and a little about the person. This is called an introduction. An *introduction* is a way to help people meet each other.

You may introduce people sometimes. You may introduce a new friend to your family. You may introduce a new friend to someone you already know. Introductions are easy when you follow a few rules.

• Look at the pictures to see how Jerry introduced his new friend Sam to his sister Peg.

Jerry did a good job of introducing Sam to Peg. Jerry told Peg a little bit about Sam in the introduction. He also told Sam who Peg was.

Talking About Introductions

1. Imagine you have brought a new friend home to introduce to your family. Your friend's name is Amy. She has just moved to your neighborhood from another town. You are going to introduce Amy to your brother Bob.

2. Imagine there is a new student in your class. His name is Tim. He has just moved to your town from another state. Introduce him to the class.

3. Imagine there is a program at your school today. Introduce Marvin the Magician to the audience.

Would you like to run a supermarket? You will have many jobs to do. Writing and speaking skills will be important. Sometimes you will need to order food. You must be able to write orders that are easy to understand. Many people will work for you. You must give them clear directions. People who shop in your store will ask many questions. You will have to answer each question.

Careers

Thank-You Notes

Thinking About Thank-You Notes

You can write a paragraph for many reasons. Imagine you went to a birthday party. You want to thank the person who invited you. You could write a paragraph thanking the person. That paragraph is part of a thank-you note.

- Look at this thank-you note.

Notice the parts of the thank-you note. The *date* shows when the note was written. The *greeting* shows to whom the note was written. The *paragraph* thanks the person for what was done or given. The *closing* says "good-by" to the person. The *name* shows who wrote the note.

Talking About Thank-You Notes

Read the thank-you note above.

1. What is the main idea sentence?
2. Is the first word indented?
3. How many detail sentences are there?
4. Where are commas used in the note?

A Class Thank-You Note

Thinking About Thank-You Notes

Your class is going to write a thank-you note together. Pretend that a bus driver visited your class. Now you want to thank her for coming. Your teacher can write your thank-you note on the board.

Writing a Thank-You Note

1. Your thank-you note will begin with today's date.

2. Choose a name to go in the greeting.

3. Start your paragraph with this sentence: *Thank you for visiting our class.*

4. Think of a sentence that tells about what the person does.

5. Think of two more sentences that tell what you learned from the person.

6. For the closing, use *Your friends,*.

7. For the name use ____ *'s class.* Put your teacher's name in the blank.

Practicing a Thank-You Note

Thinking About Your Thank-You Note

Now you are going to write a thank-you note. Pretend you have an Uncle Ted who has given you the money to buy a bicycle. In the paragraph of your thank-you note, you want to thank him for the money. You also want to describe the bicycle and tell him why you like it.

Writing Your Thank-You Note

Word Bank

I
bicycle
speeds
tires
house
store
park

1. Write today's date at the top of your note.
2. Write the greeting: *Dear Uncle Ted,*.
3. Start your paragraph with this sentence: *Thank you for the money to buy a bicycle.*
4. Write a sentence describing the color of the bicycle.
5. Write a sentence telling what you like best about the bike. Use the Word Bank.
6. Write two more sentences telling about places where you can ride.
7. For the closing, write *Love,*.
8. Write your first name.

Edit Your Thank-You Note

Read your thank-you note. Think about these questions.

1. Do your detail sentences tell about the main idea?
2. Did you use any pronouns? Which ones did you use?
3. Are the date, greeting, closing, and your name in the right places?
4. Did you indent the first word in the paragraph?
5. Did you use capital letters, commas, and periods correctly?

Correct your mistakes. If you need to, write your paragraph again.

Editing Symbols

≡ make a capital letter
¶ indent
✄ take out
∧ add

A Thank-You Note

Prewriting Thank-you notes are often written to people who help you in special ways. Imagine your class has just taken a trip to the zoo. Mrs. Brown was your guide. She helped your class during the trip. She showed you many animals and told you interesting things about them.

Plan a thank-you note to Mrs. Brown. Jot down notes that answer these questions: What animals did you see? What animal did you like best? Why did you like it?

Writing Write a thank-you note to Mrs. Brown. Use your notes to help you. Be sure to tell her what you liked best about the trip and why you liked it.

Editing Use the questions and the editing symbols above to edit your paragraph.

Unit Review

Use the special signs to write each sentence correctly. *pages 108–109*

1. a dentist fixes teeth

2. who is your dentist

3. what a big chair he has

4. can we go now

Write each sentence. Draw a line between the subject part and the predicate part. Draw one line under each noun. Draw two lines under each verb. *pages 110–113*

5. The girl cuts the grass.

6. A boy waters the plants.

7. The boy paints a fence.

8. The children plant beans.

Look at the underlined words. Write the correct pronoun to take their place. *pages 116–117*

9. <u>Rudy</u> cleans his room.

_____ sweeps the floor.

10. <u>Diane</u> makes her bed.

_____ dusts her chair.

11. <u>Tim and Ann</u> jump rope.

_____ sing a song.

12. <u>The day</u> is very cool.

_____ is dark.

Use the correct verb in each sentence. Write the verb. *pages 118–119*

13. You _____ music.   (teach, teaches)

14. I _____ the drums.   (play, plays)

15. She _____ to take lessons.   (want, wants)

16. He _____ very fast   (learn, learns)

Read each pair of sentences. Write the second sentence using the correct pronoun. *pages 120–121*

17. Janet made breakfast.

_____ brother helped.   (Her, Their)

18. Glen was hungry.

_____ plate was full.   (Our, His)

19. I was not hungry.

_____ plate was not full.   (My, Your)

20. Glen and I cleaned up.

_____ jobs are done.   (Our, Your)

Write each sentence. Put quotation marks and commas where they belong. *pages 122–123*

21. Lou whispered The baby finally fell asleep.
22. Ken answered You are a good babysitter.
23. Lou added That baby sure tired me out.
24. Ken said Look at all the toys on the floor.
25. Ken declared I will help you clean up.

Now you will write a thank-you note. *pages 132–135*

The following are the parts of a thank-you note. The parts are not in order. Put the parts in the right order. Then write the thank-you note.

a. Your friend,
b. Dear Maria,
c. Sally
d. October 19, 19 __
e.   Thank you for the books you gave me. I have already started the first book. The story is interesting so far. The pictures are also nice.

A *play* is a story that is acted out. The people in a play have conversations. This story is part of a book called <u>The Adventures of Tom Sawyer</u> by Samuel Clemens. Clemens grew up in Hannibal, Missouri. Read the play carefully.

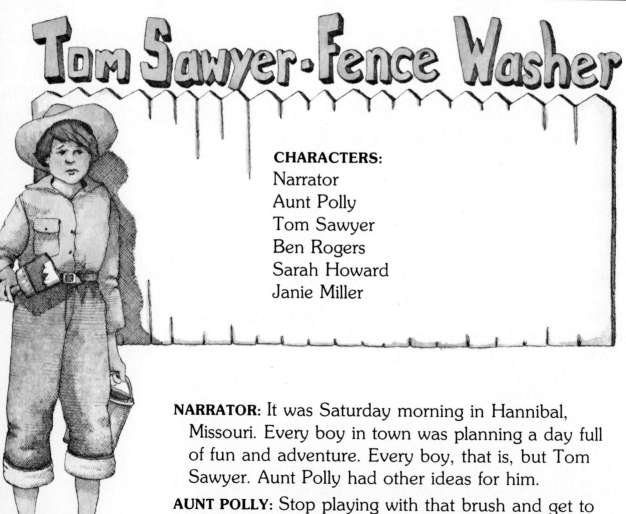

Tom Sawyer · Fence Washer

CHARACTERS:
Narrator
Aunt Polly
Tom Sawyer
Ben Rogers
Sarah Howard
Janie Miller

NARRATOR: It was Saturday morning in Hannibal, Missouri. Every boy in town was planning a day full of fun and adventure. Every boy, that is, but Tom Sawyer. Aunt Polly had other ideas for him.

AUNT POLLY: Stop playing with that brush and get to work, Tom Sawyer! I expect you to have that fence whitewashed by the time I get back from town.

TOM SAWYER: Yes, Aunt Polly. (*Aunt Polly leaves. Tom looks at the huge fence before him and sighs.*)

TOM: There must be an easy way to do this job.

NARRATOR: Tom began to whitewash. Just then his friend Ben Rogers came walking by. Suddenly Tom got an idea.

BEN ROGERS: It sure is beautiful day to go swimming. Too bad you have to work, Tom.

TOM: Who's working, Ben?

BEN: Why, you are! Don't you call whitewashing a fence work?

TOM: Well, I suppose some people might call it work. But I haven't had so much fun in a long time.

BEN: You mean you *like* it?

TOM: I sure do. It isn't every day a boy gets a chance to whitewash a fence. (*Tom begins to whistle as he works. Ben looks surprised.*)

BEN: Say, Tom, let me whitewash a little.

TOM: Oh, I don't know, Ben. Aunt Polly's awfully particular about this fence.

BEN: Oh, come on, Tom. I'll be careful. I promise.

TOM: I'd like to Ben, but—

BEN: I'll give you this apple I have in my pocket.

TOM: (*taking the apple*) Well, maybe just for a bit.

BEN: (*taking the brush*) Gee, thanks Tom! (*Ben whitewashes and Tom eats the apple. Sarah Howard and Janie Miller enter.*)

SARAH HOWARD: Poor Ben! He has to work today!

BEN: I don't *have* to work. Tom let me.

JANIE MILLER: He *what*?

BEN: I gave him my apple and he let me whitewash.

SARAH: You must be crazy!

BEN: I am not crazy. It isn't every day a boy gets a chance to whitewash a fence. Right, Tom?

TOM: Right, Ben. Now why don't you go on about your business. You're spoiling Ben's fun. (*Sarah and Janie stare at Tom. Then they stare at Ben.*)

SARAH: Hey, Tom, how about giving me a try at whitewashing?

JANIE: Me too!

TOM: Gee, I'd like to but—

SARAH: I'll give you my kite!

JANIE: I'll give you my pet frog!

TOM: Well, I suppose Ben could use a little rest . . .

NARRATOR: So Sarah and Janie took their turns whitewashing the fence. In a few hours the job was done. The painters left just as Aunt Polly arrived home.

AUNT POLLY: Well, I'll be! Tom Sawyer, I'm surprised!

TOM: (*smiling*) Oh, it wasn't so hard a job.

AUNT POLLY: It wasn't?

TOM: No, not after my friends taught me a funny thing. The only difference between work and play is how you look at it.

AUNT POLLY: I must say, Tom, sometimes you say the strangest things!

—*Steven Otfinoski*

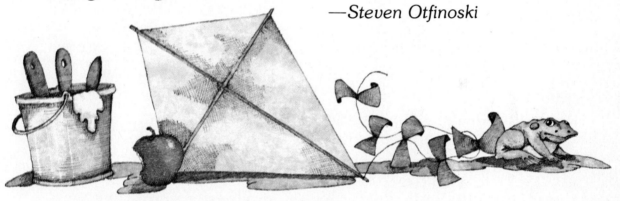

Creative Activities

1. Six students can act out the play in class. Bring the things that are needed, such as a brush and an apple. Practice the play before presenting it to the class.

2. **Creative Writing** Think about the time when you had the most fun ever. Write a paragraph that tells what you did. Tell when and where the action took place.

Read the groups of words in each pair. Write the group of words that is a sentence. *pages 2–3*

1. A dog.
A dog chased a cat.

2. A cat climbed a tree.
A cat.

3. A bird.
A bird caught a worm.

4. An owl slept all day.
An owl.

Read each sentence. Write **telling** if it is a telling sentence. Write **question** if it is a question sentence. Write **exclamation** if it is an exclamation sentence. *pages 4–5*

5. Ana walked to town.
6. Did she take her dog?
7. How long the walk was!

8. Ana saw two cats.
9. How pretty they were!
10. Did Ana go home?

Some special signs are missing in each sentence. Write each sentence correctly. *pages 6–7*

11. a bird made a nest
12. does the bird sing
13. the bird has feathers

14. how red the feathers are
15. does the bird fly
16. how high it flies

Add words to the subject part of the first two sentences. Add words to the predicate part of the last two sentences. Then write each sentence. *pages 14–15*

17. The cat watched.
18. The squirrels ran.

19. Tom and I followed.
20. The squirrels climbed.

Mid-Year Review

Write the nouns. Write **singular** if the noun is
singular. Write **plural** if the noun is plural. *pages 40-41*

21. Birds sing songs.   **24.** Boys read books.
22. A boy hit a ball.   **25.** Dogs chased sticks.
23. A girl rode a bike.   **26.** A cat chased a toy.

Write the plural form of each singular noun. *pages 42-44*

27. bat   **29.** tooth   **31.** fly
28. box   **30.** party   **32.** wish

Change the underlined word to tell what kind of
work the person does. Write the second sentence
with the new word. *page 45*

33. Amy <u>sings</u> well.   Amy is a ___.
34. Robin <u>teaches</u> school.   Robin is a ___.
35. Joan <u>writes</u> books.   Joan is a ___.
36. Juan <u>builds</u> houses.   Juan is a ___.

Write each noun. Write **proper** if the noun is a
proper noun. Write **common** if it is a common noun. *pages 48-49*

37. Ed flew to Texas.   **40.** Ed went to Trees Road.
38. A car went to Dallas.   **41.** Miyo waved at Ed.
39. Cows stood by the road.   **42.** Miyo opened the door.

Write each name and address correctly. *pages 50-53*

43.
| ms judith s levine |
| 2 astor court |
| augusta maine 04330 |

44.
| miss noreen sullivan |
| 280 beacon street |
| provo utah 84601 |

Write each date correctly. *pages 50–53*

45. September 9 1980   **48.** June 12 1981
46. November 10 1982   **49.** March 6 1982
47. October 14 1982   **50.** January 18 1979

Read each sentence. Write the verb in the present. *pages 78–79*

51. Christine ____ a tree.   (climb)
52. Christine ____ a tiny bird.   (see)
53. The tiny bird ____ on a tiny twig.   (sit)
54. Christine and Leo ____ for a nest.   (look)
55. They ____ a squirrel.   (find)
56. They ____ the squirrel.   (watch)

Read each sentence. Write the verb in the past. *pages 84–85*

57. Holly ____ a butterfly.   (chase)
58. The butterfly ____ away.   (hurry)
59. Leo ____ the dog.   (wash)
60. The children ____ some sandwiches.   (carry)
61. They ____ their lunch.   (pack)
62. The boys ____ the dishes.   (dry)

Write each sentence. Draw a line between the subject part and the predicate part.   *pages 110–111*

63. The farmer gave us a chicken.
64. The chicken ran around the yard.
65. The children fed the chicken.
66. The chicken followed the children.

Mid-Year Review

Write each sentence. Draw one line under each noun. Draw two lines under each verb. *pages 112–113*

67. Hao arrived in Paris

68. Ann opened her window.

69. A dog barked at Tom.

70. The women walked by.

Complete each sentence that has a blank. Write the pronoun. *pages 116–117, 120–121*

71. John grows a garden.
_____ planted daisies.

72. Maria runs a shop.
_____ sells hats.

73. The rain falls.
_____ floods the street.

74. Farmers clean the barn.
_____ feed animals, too.

75. The children listen to a ghost story.
_____ teacher reads the story.   (Their, Its)

76. _____ voice is low.   (Its, Her)

77. _____ sound scares William.   (Its, Their)

78. _____ eyes get bigger.   (Our, His)

Write the correct verb for each sentence. *pages 118–119*

79. She _____ a tractor.   (drive, drives)

80. They _____ bridges.   (build, builds)

81. He _____ watches.   (repair, repairs)

82. I _____ in a group.   (sing, sings)

Write each sentence. Add punctuation and capital letters where they belong. *pages 122–123*

83. Mother called where is Tommy?

84. Julie answered he is playing in the yard

85. Mother said please tell him to come in

86. Julie replied I'll call him right now.

GEYSER IN YELLOWSTONE NATIONAL PARK, WYOMING

Grammar and Related Language Skills

Review of Nouns
Possessive Nouns
Building Sentences
Capitalizing Proper Nouns

Practical Communication

STUDY AND REFERENCE SKILLS
Using a Dictionary

COMPOSITION
Writing a Friendly Letter

Creative Expression

A Poem

Nature is very beautiful. Have you ever listened to the rain or watched it snow? Have you seen an exciting picture of a mountain, a desert, or an ocean? What speaking and writing skills would help you describe your experiences with nature? What listening skills would help you understand another person's experiences?

147

Reviewing Nouns

You have learned that nouns are naming words. Words like *child*, *forest*, and *tree* are nouns.

A **noun** is a word that names a person, a place, or a thing.

You know that nouns can name one or more than one thing. The noun *flower* names one thing. The noun *flowers* names more than one thing.

A **singular noun** is a noun that names one person, place, or thing.

A **plural noun** is a noun that names more than one person, place, or thing. Most plural nouns have **-s** or **-es** endings.

You have learned about different kinds of nouns. The noun *girl* names any girl. The noun *Nancy* names a special girl.

A **common noun** is a noun that names any person, place, or thing.

A **proper noun** is a noun that names a special person, place, or thing. Each important word in a proper noun begins with a capital letter.

• Read each sentence. Then read each noun. Is it singular or plural? Is it a common noun or a proper noun?

David went to Jones Beach.   The ocean had big waves.

Talk About It

Read these sentences. Find each noun. Is the noun singular or plural? Is it a common noun or a proper noun?

1. Carla gathers shells.   **3.** A crab crawls away.
2. A shell lies in the sand.   **4.** Sand Beach looks clean.

Skills Practice

Read these sentences. Write each noun. Write **singular** if the noun is singular. Write **plural** if the noun is plural.

1. Two boys see a fish.   **4.** A girl swims.
2. The fish has blue eyes.   **5.** The girl sees big rocks.
3. The fish has a blue tail.   **6.** The rocks hide a fish.

Write each sentence correctly. Use a capital letter to begin each important word in a proper noun.

7. Our class saw mrs. lee.   **10.** A dog sees juan lopez.
8. Does peter swim often?   **11.** Sometimes mary swims.
9. Pilar lives on main street.   **12.** Did mr. arias see a fish?

Writing Sentences

Pretend you are playing at the beach.

1. Think of a singular noun. Use it in a sentence.
2. Think of a plural noun. Use it in a sentence.
3. Think of a proper noun. Use it in a sentence.

Sample Answers **1.** boys, plural; fish, singular **7.** Our class saw Mrs. Lee.

Possessive Nouns

Read this sentence.

A *turtle's shell* makes a good house.

When you talk about a *turtle's shell,* you are talking about something that *belongs to* a turtle. You use a special form of the noun *turtle* to show that the turtle has a shell. The word *turtle's* is called a possessive noun.

A **possessive noun** is a noun that names who or what has something.

● Read each sentence. Find the possessive noun.

The snake's skin shines in the sun.
The duck's feathers are white.
The frog's mouth opened wide.
A fish's tail waved in the water.

Talk About It

Read each sentence. What is the possessive noun?

1. Linda's snake lived under a rock.
2. Now the box is the snake's home.
3. Andy's frog jumps high in the air.
4. The frog's back has green spots.

Skills Practice

Write each sentence. Draw one line under the possessive noun.

1. Mr. Chin's mouse has a long tail.
2. The mouse's fur is white.
3. Mrs. Brown's fish swims in a bowl.
4. The fish's mother lived in a pond.
5. We found a robin's nest.
6. A branch held the bird's nest.
7. The robin's nest had three eggs.
8. A little bird's head appeared.
9. We heard the baby's cry.
10. The bird's mother will bring food soon.

Sample Answer 1. Mr. Chin's mouse has a long tail.

Singular Possessive Nouns

You know that possessive nouns name who or what has something.

Ellen's horse won the race.

Ellen is a singular noun that names one person. To show that something belongs to Ellen, you write *Ellen's*. You add an *apostrophe* and *-s ('s)*.

Ellen + 's ———→ Ellen's

● Look at each pair of nouns. What was added to each singular noun to make it possessive?

sister   Jason   bird
sister's   Jason's   bird's

Add an **apostrophe** and **-s** (**'s**) to write the possessive of most singular nouns.

Talk About It

What is the possessive form of each singular noun? Use each possessive noun in a sentence.

1. fish   **2.** hen   **3.** Bonnie   **4.** brother

Skills Practice

Write the possessive form of each singular noun.

1. goose   **3.** Glen   **5.** squirrel   **7.** boy
2. Diane   **4.** bug   **6.** girl   **8.** owl

Sample Answer **1.** goose's

Plural Possessive Nouns

You can make plural nouns possessive, too.

The farmers' tractor stopped.

The word *farmers* is a plural noun that ends in *s*.
To show that something belongs to the farmers, you
write *farmers'*. You add an *apostrophe* (').

farmers + '──→ farmers'

- Look at each pair of nouns. What was added to
each plural noun to make it possessive?

ducks	ants	daughters
ducks'	ants'	daughters'

> Add an **apostrophe** (') to write the
> possessive of most plural nouns.

Talk About It

What is the possessive form of each plural noun?
Use each possessive noun in a sentence.

1. girls   **2.** teachers   **3.** skunks   **4.** horses

Skills Practice

Write the possessive of each plural noun.

1. animals   **3.** doctors   **5.** rabbits   **7.** frogs
2. boys   **4.** raccoons   **6.** friends   **8.** sons

Sample Answer **1.** animals'

Possessive Nouns in Sentences

You use possessive nouns to name who or what has something. Possessive nouns can be singular or plural.

The <u>boy's dogs</u> bark.   The <u>boys' dogs</u> bark.

Boy's is a singular possessive noun. It shows that one person has the dogs.
Boys' is a plural possessive noun. It shows that more than one person has the dogs.

- Read each sentence. Find the possessive noun. Is it singular or plural? What ending was added to make the noun possessive?

The girls followed the animal's tracks.
They led to a bear's cave.
The girls' brother called them.
He found a raccoon's tracks.

Talk About It

Complete each sentence. Decide if the noun in ( )
is singular or plural. Then use the possessive form
of the noun in the blank.

1. The ____ cat has two kittens.   (boy)
2. They sleep in the ____ basket.   (cat)
3. The ____ mother feeds them.   (kittens)
4. The ____ friend took a kitten.   (girls)

Skills Practice

Decide if the noun in ( ) is singular or plural. Use
the possessive form of the noun in the blank. Write
the sentence.

1. The ____ dog chased a rabbit.   (boys)
2. The ____ tail wagged.   (dog)
3. The dog ran to the ____ home.   (rabbit)
4. The rabbit hid in the ____ tent.   (girls)
5. The boys saw a ____ nest in a tree.   (squirrel)
6. Some squirrels ate the ____ popcorn.   (boys)
7. A squirrel ran across a ____ tent.   (girl)

Writing Sentences

Pretend you and a friend are walking in a forest.
Think of some animals you might see. Write two
sentences to tell about them. Use a possessive noun
in each sentence.

Sample Answers **1.** The boys' dog chased a rabbit. **2.** The dog's tail wagged.

Skills Review

Read these sentences. Write each noun. Write **singular** if the noun is singular. Write **plural** if the noun is plural.

1. The rabbit has long ears.
2. Rabbits eat green plants.
3. The fox chases the squirrel.
4. Squirrels hide nuts in trees.
5. The owl lives in a tree.
6. Owls fly at night.

Write each sentence correctly. Use a capital letter to begin each important word in a proper noun.

7. Did mr. black pick some flowers?
8. My aunt gave the pretty rock to mrs. ramos.
9. Does jane like animals?
10. My sister visited a friend in new mexico.
11. The kitten belongs to barry.

Read these sentences. Write the possessive nouns.

12. Paul's dog barks.
13. He pats the dog's head.
14. The dog runs to Jill's house.
15. She rides a friend's horse.
16. The horse's legs are white.

Write the possessive form of each singular noun.

17. Jack
18. raccoon
19. puppy
20. girl

Write the possessive form of each plural noun.

21. kittens   **23.** owls
22. boys   **24.** bears

Decide if the noun in ( ) is singular or plural. Use the possessive form of the noun in the blank. Write the possessive form of each noun.

25. We found an ___ tracks. (animal)
26. They led to the ___ tent. (boys)
27. A ___ paws made the track. (raccoon)
28. The raccoon ate the ___ popcorn. (girls)
29. A ___ bark scared the raccoon. (dog)

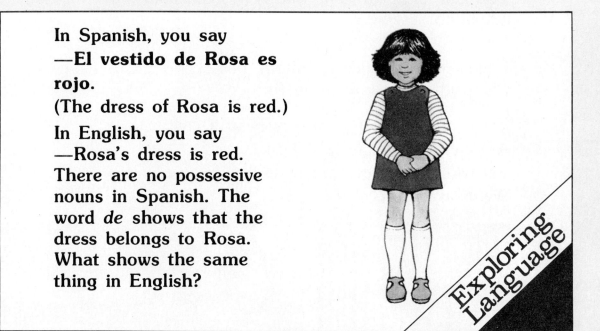

In Spanish, you say
—**El vestido de Rosa es rojo.**
(The dress of Rosa is red.)

In English, you say
—Rosa's dress is red.
There are no possessive nouns in Spanish. The word *de* shows that the dress belongs to Rosa. What shows the same thing in English?

Exploring Language

Possessive Nouns with Special Endings

Some plural nouns do not form the plural in the usual way. They do not end in *s* or *es*.

● Read each pair of nouns below. Which noun is singular? Which noun is plural? Look at how the spelling in the plural noun changes.

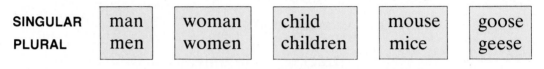

SINGULAR	man	woman	child	mouse	goose
PLURAL	men	women	children	mice	geese

The plural nouns in the boxes do not end in *s*. Suppose you want to show that something belongs to the men. You add an *apostrophe* and *-s ('s)*.

The men's voices are loud.

All the plural nouns above work the same way. You add an *apostrophe* and *-s ('s)* to make the nouns possessive.

● Read each sentence. Find the possessive noun. How was each possessive noun formed?

The children's pet mouse lives in a cage.
A kitten ate the mice's food.
The women's geese are in the lake.
We hear the geese's cries.

Talk About It

Complete each sentence. Look at the noun in ( ).
Use the possessive form of the noun in the blank.

1. The ___ father bought a puppy.   (child)
2. The puppy played with the ___ dog.   (man)
3. The ___ dogs liked each other.   (men)

Skills Practice

Look at the noun in ( ). Use the possessive
form of the noun in the blank. Write each
sentence.

1. The ___ bird sang a song.   (woman)
2. The ___ mother fed the birds.   (children)
3. A young ___ feathers are soft.   (goose)
4. The ___ dog found a fox.   (men)
5. The fox tried to hide in a ___ hole.   (mouse)
6. The ___ friend called the dog.   (child)
7. We kept bags of seed in the ___ barn.   (women)
8. We saw the ___ nest in the barn.   (mice)
9. The seed was for the ___ geese.   (man)
10. The mice ate the ___ food.   (geese)

Sample Answers 1. The woman's bird sang a song.
2. The children's mother fed the birds.

Building Sentences

You can put together sentences like these to make one sentence.

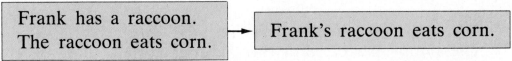

Frank has a raccoon.
The raccoon eats corn.

Frank's raccoon eats corn.

The new sentence tells the same thing. But it does not use the same words over again. You use a possessive noun in the new sentence.

- Read the two groups of words again. What word in the new sentence shows that Frank has a raccoon? What kind of word is it?

Talk About It

Read each pair of sentences. Put them together to make one sentence. What possessive noun did you use in the new sentence?

1. Ned has a pony
The pony has spots.

2. The boys have a wagon.
The wagon has wheels.

Skills Practice

Read each pair of sentences. Put them together to make one sentence. Write the new sentence.

1. Pam has a fish.
The fish lives in a bowl.

2. Elisa has a kitten.
The kitten walks slowly.

3. The girls have horses.
The horses trot quickly.

4. Mr. Li has mice.
The mice make noise.

Sample Answer **1.** Pam's fish lives in a bowl.

Compound Words

Words change all the time. New words are made up. Some old words are no longer used. One way to make a new word is to put two words together. A *compound word* is a word made up of two other words.

homework ———→ home + work
tablecloth ———→ table + cloth

- Read the two words that make up each compound word. They give you an idea of what the compound word means.

Homework is work you do at home.
A tablecloth is a cloth you put on a table.

Talk About It

What two words make up each compound word?
Use them to tell the meaning of the compound word.

1. doghouse   **2.** football   **3.** birthday   **4.** spaceship

Skills Practice

Find the two words that make up each compound word. Use them in the blanks to tell the meaning of the compound word. Then write each sentence.

1. A basketball is a ____ you throw through a ____ .
2. A sailboat is a ____ with a ____ .
3. A raincoat is a ____ you wear in the ____ .
4. A lunchroom is a ____ where you eat ____ .

Sample Answer 1. A basketball is a ball you throw through a basket.

Capitalizing Days, Months, and Special Days

You know that you should start each proper noun with a capital letter. The names of days, months, and special days are proper nouns. They begin with capital letters.

DAYS OF THE WEEK	MONTHS OF THE YEAR	SPECIAL DAYS
Sunday	January	New Year's Day
Monday	February	Lincoln's Birthday
Tuesday	March	Washington's Birthday
Wednesday	April	April Fools' Day
Thursday	May	Mother's Day
Friday	June	Father's Day
Saturday	July	Independence Day
	August	Halloween
	September	Thanksgiving
	October	Labor Day
	November	
	December	

- Look at the list of special days above. Which names have apostrophes? Can you think of other special days? How do you write them?

Talk About It

Read these sentences. What words should begin
with capital letters?

1. The first day in january is new year's day.
2. Is labor day always on monday?
3. Which day in july is independence day?
4. When is washington's birthday?

Skills Practice

Write each sentence correctly. Use a capital letter
to begin each important word in a proper noun.

1. My family went on vacation in august.
2. Is lincoln's birthday in february?
3. Do you go to school on saturday?
4. We go to the library every tuesday.
5. I dress up on halloween.
6. Do you like april fools' day?
7. We have mother's day in may.
8. Is father's day in june?
9. Our thanksgiving day is always on thursday.
10. We played outside on sunday.

Writing Sentences

Think about your three favorite special days. Write
a sentence to tell what you do on each special day.

Sample Answer 1. My family went on vacation in August.

SkillsReview

Look at the noun in ( ). Use the possessive form of the noun in the blank. Write the possessive form of each noun.

1. The ____ cow gives milk.   (woman)
2. The ____ horses eat hay.   (men)
3. The ____ cat sleeps in the barn.   (child)
4. The ____ babies are tiny.   (mouse)
5. The ____ dog wants a bone.   (children)
6. The ____ chickens laid many eggs.   (women)

Read each pair of sentences. Put them together to make one sentence. Write the new sentence.

7. Mark has a tent.
   The tent keeps out the rain.

8. Mr. Silver has a dog.
   The dog chases rabbits.

9. The boys have friends.
   The friends like to swim.

10. Ms. Olson has a pond.
    The pond has many fish.

11. The girls have a bird.
    The bird can talk.

12. Ann has a cat.
    The cat lives in the barn.

Find the two words that make up each compound word. Use them in the blanks to tell the meaning of the compound word. Then write each sentence.

13. A <u>tablecloth</u> is a ___ you put on a ___ .
14. A <u>doghouse</u> is a ___ for a ___ .
15. A <u>sailboat</u> is a ___ with a ___ .
16. A <u>football</u> is a ___ you kick with your ___ .
17. A <u>spaceship</u> is a ___ that goes into ___ .

Write each sentence correctly. Use a capital letter to begin each important word in a proper noun.

18. We have chicken for dinner on wednesday.
19. It can be very windy in march.
20. I bought my bike in december.
21. We have thanksgiving day in november.
22. It often rains in april.
23. We went on vacation in september.
24. They stayed home on sunday.
25. Is halloween in october?

Read this verse. What does the verse tell you about the different months of the year?

Thirty days have September,
April, June, and November,
All the rest have thirty-one,
Except for February alone,
Which has but twenty-eight in time
Till Leap Year gives it twenty-nine.

Exploring Language

Guide Words in a Dictionary

Alphabetical order in a dictionary helps you find words quickly. The dictionary has another way to help you find words. There are two words at the top of almost every dictionary page. These two words are guide words. *Guide Words* tell the first word and the last word on a dictionary page. All the words on a dictionary page must come between the guide words.

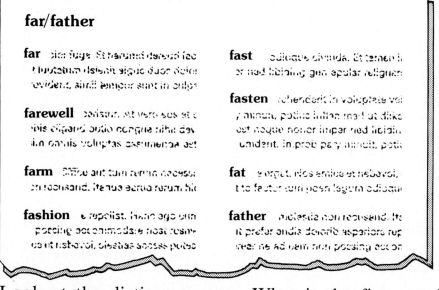

far/father

far ...

farewell ...

farm ...

fashion ...

fast ...

fasten ...

fat ...

father ...

• Look at the dictionary page. What is the first word on the page? What is the last word? What are the guide words?

• Look at these guide words. Which guide words should you use to find the word *clown*?

cloth/club   **coal/cube**

You should use the guide words **cloth/club.** The word *clown* comes between these guide words.

Talk About It

Here is a part of a dictionary page. What are the guide words? Which of the words below would you find on this page?

telephone/ten

1. teeth
2. television
3. tell
4. temper
5. temperature
6. test

Skills Practice

Read each word at the left. Does it come between the guide words in **a** or **b**? Write the letter of the correct pair of words.

1. doctor   a. **dock/dollar**
            b. **defend/do**

2. shook   a. **shoe/short**
            b. **sick/sign**

3. manner   a. **magic/main**
            b. **manage/many**

4. across   a. **ache/act**
            b. **about/accept**

The guide words on a dictionary page are **day/defend.** Which of these words would you find on the page? Write the words.

5. daze   7. debt   9. deed   11. defend

6. dead   8. deck   10. defeat   12. delay

Sample Answer 1. a

Dictionary: Word Meaning

You find new words in many different places. You may read new words in books. Sometimes you hear people use new words when they talk. A dictionary can help you find out what the words mean.

- Look at this dictionary page. Find the word *dodo*. What does *dodo* mean?

---

do/dot

do   Susan helped Mary *do* her homework.

doctor   Someone who takes care of sick people and makes them well. Sara's father took her to the *doctor* when she was sick.

dodo   A kind of large bird that lived a long time ago. The *dodo* had a big hooked bill and a short tail of curly feathers. Its wings were so small that the bird could not fly.

dog   An animal that has four legs, fur, and barks. Leroy has a *dog* as a pet.

doll   A toy that looks like a baby, a child, or an older person.

dollar   A piece of money. It is the same as one hundred cents.

donkey   An animal that looks very much like a small horse. It sometimes carries or pulls things. The *donkey* pulled the wagon.

dot   A small, round mark or spot. This dress has many *dots*.

Sometimes you find an example sentence after a word meaning. The *example sentence* shows you how the word is used.

- Use the dictionary page above. Find the word *donkey*. What does *donkey* mean? Read the example sentence for *donkey*.

Talk About It

Find these words on the sample dictionary page.
Tell the meaning of each word.

1. dollar   **2.** doctor   **3.** doll

Complete each sentence. Choose the correct word
from the sample dictionary page.

4. Ms. Ramos gave me a ___ for helping her.
5. That ___ looks like a real baby.

Skills Practice

Find these words on the sample dictionary page.
Write the meaning of each word.

1. dot   **2.** dog   **3.** do

Look at each picture. Find the words on the sample
dictionary page that name what each picture shows.
Write the words.

4.   **5.**   **6.**

Complete each sentence. Choose the correct word
from the sample dictionary page. Write the word.

7. Pete's ___ always barks at me.
8. The ___ carried heavy boxes.
9. Don helped me ___ a trick.
10. My new dress has many blue ___ .

Sample Answers **1.** A small, round mark or spot. **7.** dog

A Friendly Letter

Most people like being with their friends. They want to tell about interesting things that have happened to them. They also like to hear what their friends are doing.

Sometimes friends move away. But you still like to share news with them. That is why you write friendly letters. A *friendly letter* is a way to tell your friends what you are doing.

- Look at the letter Mark wrote to a friend who had moved away.

> 76 Newton Avenue
> Atlanta, Georgia, 30304   ← heading
> November 9, 19—
>
> Dear Jane,   ← greeting
>
>   I hope you are having fun in your new home. I am doing many things here. My brother took me fishing last Saturday. On Monday I gave a report in school. Next week our whole family is going to the circus. I am looking forward to it.   ← paragraph
>
>   Your friend,   ← closing
>   Mark   ← name

In the paragraph Mark told about things that happened to him. He said the same things he might say if he were talking to his friend in person.

A friendly letter and a thank-you note have similar parts. Mark's letter has a *heading, a greeting, a paragraph, a closing,* and the writer's *name.*

Remember what each part of the letter does.

Heading   Shows where and when the letter was written
Greeting   Shows to whom the letter was written
Paragraph   Tells the person something
Closing   Says "good-by" to the person
Name   Shows who wrote the letter

Commas are used in the date, greeting, and closing. Remember to indent the first word of the paragraph.

Talking About a Letter

Read the letter on the other page.
1. Who wrote the letter?
2. What was the date?
3. Whose name was in the greeting?
4. What was the closing?
5. What did the writer talk about in the letter?
6. Where were commas used in the letter?

Writing a Letter

When you write a friendly letter, you need to know what order the parts come in. The parts of a friendly letter are listed below. They are not in the order you would write them. Write the parts in the correct order.

| name | heading | greeting |
| paragraph | closing | |

A Class Letter

Your class is going to write a friendly letter together. Pretend that someone in your class is ill. The person has been out of school for a week. Your class wants to write to him or her and tell what is happening in school.

When you finish writing a letter, you need to address an envelope to send your letter. Here is the way an envelope is addressed:

Mark Miller
146 Wabash Avenue
Columbus, Ohio 43209

← return address

Miss Jane Taylor
88 River Road
Columbus, Ohio 43207

← mailing address

The middle of the envelope has the *mailing address*. This is the name and address of the person who will get the letter.

The top left corner of the envelope has the *return address*. It shows the writer's name and address. If the post office cannot find the house of the person to whom the letter is written, they will return the letter to the writer.

Remember to use capital letters for the names of people, streets, cities, and states. There is a comma between the city and state. The ZIP code follows the state.

Writing a Letter

Your teacher will write the letter and envelope on the board.

1. Begin the letter with the heading.
2. Use the greeting *Dear Bill,*. Where should it be written?
3. Start your paragraph with this sentence: *We hope you are feeling better.*
4. Think of one sentence that tells about what happened in class yesterday.
5. Think of a sentence that tells about your homework. Think of another sentence about what will happen in class tomorrow.
6. Use the closing *Your friends,*.
7. For the name, use ____ *'s class.* Use your teacher's name in the blank.
8. Think of a mailing address and a return address for the envelope.

Careers

Forest rangers have an important job. They take care of plants and animals in our parks and forests. They watch for fires and floods. They must read books to learn how to take care of our forests. Forest rangers also must speak well. They guide people through our parks and forests. They tell the visitors about plants and animals.

Practicing a Friendly Letter

Thinking About Your Letter

Now you are going to write a friendly letter. Imagine that a friend has moved away. Write a letter to your friend about Valentine's Day or some other special day at school. Use the pictures below and the Word Bank to help write your letter.

Writing Your Letter

1. Begin your letter with the heading.
2. Use the name of your friend in the greeting. Write the word *Dear* before your friend's name. Use a comma after the name.
3. Start your paragraph with this sentence: *I had a good time on Valentine's Day.* You may also use your own sentence.
4. Write three sentences that tell about Valentine's Day at your school.
5. Use the closing *Your friend,.* Write your own name after the closing.
6. Address an envelope to your friend. Use your own name and address for the return address.

Word Bank

box
cover
paper
color
red
white
valentine

Edit Your Friendly Letter

Edit your letter and envelope. Use the questions below.

1. Did your detail sentences tell about the main idea?
2. Which possessive nouns did you use in your sentences?
3. Are the heading, greeting, closing, and name in the right places? Did you use commas correctly?
4. Did you capitalize the names of people, months, streets, cities, states, and special days?
5. Is your envelope addressed correctly?

Correct your mistakes. If you need to, write your letter and envelope again.

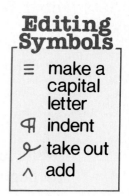

Editing Symbols

≡ make a capital letter
¶ indent
✗ take out
∧ add

INDEPENDENT WRITING
A Friendly Letter

Prewriting Friendly letters are written to tell our friends about interesting things that happen to us. Imagine that a creature from outer space landed in your backyard. Think about what you would tell a friend about this happening. Jot down some notes or words about the creature and what happened to you.

Writing Use your notes to write a friendly letter that describes the visit of a creature from outer space. Look at Mark's letter on page 170 to make sure all the parts of your letter are correct. You may want to prepare an envelope, as well.

Editing Use the check questions and the editing symbols above to edit your letter.

Unit Review

Read these sentences. Write each noun. Write
singular if the noun is singular. Write **plural** if the
noun is plural. *pages 148-149*

1. The man found a cave.
2. The cave had two cubs.
3. Two lions came to the cave.
4. The lions brought food.

Write each sentence correctly. Use a capital letter
to begin each important word in a proper noun. *pages 148-149*

5. mr. alba watched the rain.
6. He was inside lincoln school.
7. leah wanted to go outside.
8. People ran down liberty avenue.

Read these sentences. Write the possessive nouns. *pages 150-151*

9. We drove past Judy's house.
10. Maria's brother waved to us.
11. A man's dog barked at me.
12. My friend's dog barked, too.

Decide if the noun in ( ) is singular or plural. Write
the possessive form of each noun. *pages 152–155*

13. The ___ frog is green.   (boys)
14. The ___ legs are strong.   (frog)
15. The frog can jump out of the ___ box.   (girl)
16. My ___ cat saw the frog.   (friends)

Look at the noun at the end of each sentence. Write
the possessive form of each noun. *pages 158-159*

17. We found the ____ nest. (mice)
18. The ____ friends waited outside. (children)
19. I have the ____ hat. (man)
20. They touch the ____ feathers. (geese)

Read each pair of sentences. Put them together to
make one sentence. Write the new sentence. *page 160*

21. George has a kite.   22. Tami has a record.
    The kite is red.   The record broke.

Write each sentence correctly. Use a capital letter
to begin each important word in a proper noun. *pages 162-163*

23. I play on new year's day.   25. He plays tennis tuesday.
24. We go out on labor day.   26. Is halloween in october?

You are going to write a friendly letter. *pages 170-175*

27. Write the heading at the top of the letter.
28. Think of a person you want to write to. Write
    the person's name in the greeting *Dear* ____ .
29. Write a paragraph of three or four sentences.
    You might tell about something that happened
    to you or a place you visited.
30. Write the closing *Your friend.*
31. Write your name.

A Poem

How many ways did you act today? What were you like this morning? Were you as sleepy as a bear in winter? What were you like on the playground today? Were you as quick as the wind?

In just one day, you act in many different ways. You can use different words to tell about all your feelings. Many times you will use words like happy or sad or quiet. Sometimes you will compare yourself to something else. In this poem, the author describes many ways a child like you can feel.

These *Words to Think About* will help you understand the poem.

Words to Think About
suits, pleases   **bustling,** busy
knight, king's mounted soldier   **brood,** think hard

I Can Be...

It's fun to see
What I can be ...
To imagine a world
That just suits me!

I can be as quiet
as snowflakes
falling to ground.

Or,
I can be as noisy as
the bang ballons make
when they break.

I can be as shy
as a lamb that's
playing hide-and-seek.

Or,
I can be as bold
as a knight
in shining armor.

I can be as calm
and still as
a moonlit night.

Or,
I can be as lively
as a big brass band.

I can be as lazy
as a summer day.

Or,
I can be as busy as
a bustling beaver.

I can be as peaceful as
sunlight shining through
a stained-glass window.

Or,
I can be as excited
as the Fourth of July.

I can be as slow
as a tired turtle.

Or,
I can be as fast
as a rocket racing
through the sky.

I can shout and laugh
Or sit and brood —
And change the world
To fit my mood!

A. K. Roche

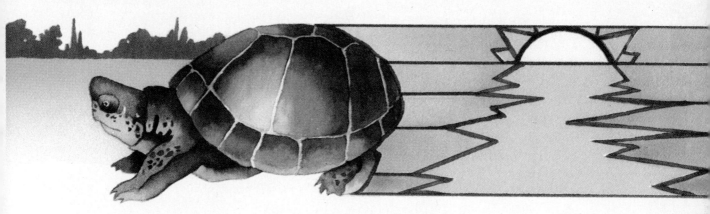

Creative Activities

1. **Creative Writing**   Words can be used to describe how you feel. Read this sentence.

   I am as <u>happy</u> as a <u>sunny</u> day.

   The word *happy* tells how the person feels. The words *sunny day* help you imagine how the person feels. In the poem "I Can Be . . . ," the author uses words to tell how he feels. He also uses words to help you imagine how he feels. Make a list of all the words in the poem that tell you how the author feels. Next to it, make a list of the words that help you imagine what the author feels. Here is an example.

   quiet   snowflakes

2. Draw a picture of something that shows how you feel. Do not draw a picture of yourself. A sunny day is a picture for a happy feeling. Think of a special feeling. Draw a special picture for it.

Grammar and
Related Language Skills

Adjectives
Adjectives That Compare
Synonyms
Antonyms
Words That Sound the Same

Practical Communication

STUDY AND REFERENCE SKILLS
Taking and Organizing Notes
COMPOSITION
Writing a Story

Creative Expression

A Story

A hobby is something you do for fun in your free time. Some people enjoy painting or drawing. Some people build model airplanes or cars for a hobby. Do you have a hobby? Hobby shops sell supplies for many hobbies. What listening and speaking skills would a hobby shop owner need?

Adjectives

Words that name people, places, or things are *nouns.* Sometimes you want to tell more about the nouns. You use special words to describe them.

- Read these sentences.

Donna has a kite.
Donna has a red kite.

The word *kite* is a noun. The word *red* describes the kite. *Red* is an *adjective*.

> An **adjective** is a word that describes a noun.

- Read each pair of sentences. The underlined word in each sentence is a noun.

The <u>boy</u> makes a kite.
The little <u>boy</u> makes a kite.

He uses <u>paper</u>.
He uses brown <u>paper</u>.

The kite has a <u>tail</u>.
The kite has a long <u>tail</u>.

They fly the kite in a <u>field</u>.
They fly the kite in a big <u>field</u>.

The second sentence in each pair has an adjective that tells more about the underlined noun. Find the adjectives.

Talk About It

Read each sentence. Find the adjective. Then find
the noun it describes.

1. I save new stamps.
2. You save old bottles.
3. She saves small coins.

4. We save round rocks.
5. He saves blue shells.
6. They save large postcards.

Skills Practice

Read each sentence. Write the adjective. Then write
the noun it describes.

1. The little girl looked.
2. She lost a green stamp.
3. It fell into a big hole.
4. A big boy found it.
5. A huge dog barked.
6. A white cat ran.

7. We save old stamps.
8. Pat reads a large book.
9. She found a blue stamp.
10. Carl drove a yellow car.
11. A small store sold coins.
12. A man bought a gold coin.

Writing Sentences

Imagine that you save rocks. Write three sentences
about your rocks. Use adjectives in your sentences.
You may use the adjectives in the box.

| round | flat | tiny | red | small | yellow |

Sample Answer 1. little, girl

More About Adjectives

You can use different adjectives to describe a noun. The adjectives in the green box tell how a person, place, or thing *looks*.

red	big	old
orange	little	new
yellow	long	clean
green	short	dirty

- Choose an adjective to complete each sentence. Describe what you see in the picture. The adjectives in the green box may help you.

I have a ____ mouse.

The mouse has a ____ tail.

The mouse lives in a ____ cage.

The mouse eats a ____ piece of cheese.

The words in the orange box are adjectives, too. They tell how a person, place, or thing *feels*.

hot	wet	bumpy
warm	dry	smooth
cold	sticky	hard
cool	sharp	soft

- Choose an adjective from the orange box to complete each sentence.

We found a ____ rock.   It fell in the ____ water.

It had a ____ edge.   You wrapped it in ____ cloth.

Here are some more adjectives.
These adjectives tell how a
person, place, or thing *sounds*,
tastes, or *smells*.

loud	low	sweet
soft	squeaky	sour
high	fresh	salty

- Choose an adjective from the blue
  box to complete each sentence.

Lisa heard a ＿＿ noise.
She smelled the ＿＿ air.
Jean tasted the ＿＿ berries.

Talk About It

Complete each sentence. Use an adjective. These
adjectives will come from all three boxes.

1. I pet the ＿＿ kitten.
2. We fed it ＿＿ milk.

3. We heard the ＿＿ dog.
4. It has a ＿＿ bark.

Skills Practice

Complete each sentence with an adjective. Write the
sentence.

1. We hit a ＿＿ ball.
2. He wore a ＿＿ cap.
3. She swung the ＿＿ bat.
4. It was a ＿＿ day.

5. We went to a ＿＿ park.
6. I swam in a ＿＿ pool.
7. You drank ＿＿ water.
8. We ate ＿＿ ice cream.

Writing Sentences

Think about one of these things. Write three sentences
telling about it. Use adjectives in your sentences.

1. Something you like

2. Your best friend

Adjectives That Compare

You know that an adjective describes a noun. A *noun* names a person, place, or thing. An *adjective* describes how the noun looks, feels, sounds, smells, or tastes.

Adjectives can also be used to compare nouns. You may have a fast model car. Your friend may have a car that is faster than yours.

- Read these sentences.

Sue found an <u>old</u> stamp.
Tom found an <u>older</u> stamp than Sue did.

In the two sentences the two stamps have been described. One is older than the other. Look at the word *old* in the second sentence. How did it change? To compare two different things, you add *-er* to an adjective.

- Now look at these sentences.

Fred saved an <u>old</u> penny.
I saved an <u>older</u> penny than Fred did.
Ruth saved the <u>oldest</u> penny of all.

The three pennies are compared by using the adjectives *old, older,* and *oldest.* How did the word *old* change in the third sentence? To compare several things, add *-est* to the adjective.

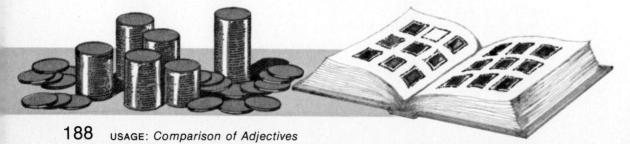

Talk About It

Complete each sentence. Choose the correct
adjective to fill each blank.

1. Ed has a new baseball card.
I have a ____ card than Ed's.   (newer, newest)
2. Hao built three small model cars.
The ____ car of all is red.   (smaller, smallest)
3. I bought the ____ airplane in the whole store.
(longer, longest)
4. Jo has a ____ plane than mine.   (shorter, shortest)
5. Kim has the ____ plane of all.   (shorter, shortest)

Skills Practice

Choose the correct adjective to fill each blank.
Then write the sentence.

1. Jay owns a small football card.
I own a ____ card than Jay's. (smaller, smallest)
2. Dad owns the ____ card of all.   (smaller, smallest)
3. Eva saved a new bottle cap.
Don saved a ____ cap than Eva's.   (newer, newest)
4. Pat saved the ____ cap of all.   (newer, newest)
5. May has the ____ dime I have ever seen.
(older, oldest)
6. Juan kept four clean rocks.
The ____ rock of all is gray.   (cleaner, cleanest)
7. I found an ____ rock than Kay did.   (older, oldest)

Sample Answer 1. I own a smaller card than Jay's.

Number Words

Sometimes you want to tell *how many* people, places, or things you are talking about. Then you use number words like *one, two, three.* Number words can be adjectives. They tell *how many.*

● Find the number word in each sentence.

I counted ten birds.
Four birds sat on the fence.
Five birds flew to the tree.
There was one bird on the grass.

Talk About It

Complete each sentence. Use a number word.

1. Rosa made ＿＿ blouses.
2. She put ＿＿ buttons on them.
3. Sam painted ＿＿ pictures.
4. He used ＿＿ colors.

Skills Practice

Complete each sentence with a number word. Write the sentence.

1. Frank baked ＿＿ cookies.
2. Ann made ＿＿ cake.
3. The boys ate ＿＿ eggs.
4. They washed ＿＿ plates.
5. I want ＿＿ pieces.
6. The girls had ＿＿ seeds.
7. They watered ＿＿ plants.
8. They pulled ＿＿ weeds.
9. Pat picked ＿＿ apples.
10. Al made ＿＿ pies.

Articles

You often use the words *a, an,* and *the* before nouns. These three words are called *articles.*

Use *an* before words that begin with vowel sounds. Use *a* before words that begin with all other sounds.

Jenny flew <u>an</u> airplane.   Brent drove <u>a</u> car.

Use *a* and *an* before singular nouns only.

Use *the* before singular or plural nouns.

Pam sailed <u>the</u> boat.   Ken rode <u>the</u> horses.

Talk About It

Choose a correct article for each sentence.

1. Ben has ___ bicycle.
2. ___ bicycle has a basket.
3. Lynn washes ___ cars.
4. She can drive ___ automobile.

Skills Practice

Complete each sentence. Use a correct article. Write the sentence.

1. Tim made ___ toy airplane.
2. He used ___ pieces of wood.
3. He carved ___ wood.
4. ___ airplane can fly.

5. Sue bought ___ kites.
6. She runs in ___ park.
7. She eats ___ orange.
8. She saves ___ apple.

Sample Answer 1. Tim made a (the) toy airplane.

Skills Review

Read each sentence. Write the adjective. Then write the noun it describes.

1. The small boy found a rock.
2. He picked up the shiny rock.
3. He put it in a large bag.
4. He collects pretty things.
5. The tall girl has a garden.

Complete each sentence with an adjective. Write the adjective.

6. We walk on the ____ beach.
7. The children like a ____ day.
8. Children play with a ____ ball.
9. They swim in the ____ water.
10. We eat ____ fruit.

Choose the correct adjective to fill each blank.
Write the adjective.

11. Joey saw a small bee.
    Rico saw a ____ bee than Joey did.
    (smaller, smallest)
12. Lu saw the ____ bee of all.
    (smaller, smallest)
13. Four large cows came to the barn.
    The ____ cow of all was brown.
    (larger, largest)

Complete each sentence with a number word. Write the number word.

14. I counted ___ mice.

15. ___ mice ate cheese.

16. I saw ___ mouse.

17. Tim has ___ papers.

18. He used ___ crayons.

19. He drew ___ pictures.

Complete each sentence. Use a correct article. Write the article.

20. Cathy has ___ puppet.

21. The puppet wears ___ old dress.

22. ___ dress has two bows.

23. Cathy tied ___ bows.

24. We built ___ doghouse.

Write a story like the one below. Leave blanks for the adjectives and nouns. Ask a friend for a list of adjectives and nouns. Do not say why you want them. Fill in the blanks with the words. See what a silly story you have written.

The _____ _____ went to the _____.
      adjective noun   noun
                                   (place)

A _____ _____ _____ went, too.
  adjective   adjective noun

They ate _____ _____ for dinner.
       adjective noun
       (color) (plural)

They drank _____ _____.
       adjective noun
              (plural)

Exploring Language

Synonyms

Jeff wrote to thank his uncle for a book.

● Read Jeff's letter.

Thank you for the nice book. It tells a nice story. I like the nice pictures. You are a nice uncle to send it to me.

Jeff used the word *nice* four times. He could have used the words *interesting, wonderful, beautiful,* or *good*. These words are *synonyms* for *nice*.

A **synonym** is a word that has nearly the same meaning as another word.

Talk About It

Read each adjective in the first column. Then find a synonym for it in the second column.

1. big   **a.** sad
2. noisy   **b.** lovely
3. pretty   **c.** loud
4. unhappy   **d.** large

Skills Practice

Use a synonym for the underlined word. Write your new sentence. You may use the words in the list above.

1. Jan has a <u>pretty</u> hat.   **4.** An <u>unhappy</u> boy fell.
2. She saw a <u>big</u> feather.   **5.** He lost a <u>bright</u> coin.
3. A <u>smart</u> man sold it.   **6.** A <u>noisy</u> horn honked.

Antonyms

● Read these pairs of sentences.

Jill has <u>long</u> hair.   The <u>clean</u> dog is Tag.
Bill has <u>short</u> hair.   The <u>dirty</u> dog is Rags.

The underlined words in each pair of sentences have opposite meanings. These words are *antonyms*.

> An **antonym** is a word that means
> the opposite of another word.

● Find the antonyms in each pair of sentences.

I drank some hot milk.   Dan has an empty glass.
You drank some cold milk.   Anita has a full glass.

Talk About It

Read each adjective in the first column. Then find an antonym for it in the second column.

1. dry   **a.** closed
2. hard   **b.** bottom
3. big   **c.** wet
4. open   **d.** soft
5. top   **e.** small

Skills Practice

Use an antonym for each underlined word. Write your new sentence. You may use the words from above.

1. I have a <u>big</u> jar.   3. It had <u>hard</u> clay in it.
2. Pat put it on a <u>top</u> shelf.   4. I keep it in a <u>dry</u> place.

Making Adjectives

Some words are made by adding an ending to another word. Many adjectives are made by adding -*y* to certain nouns.

> bump
> bump**y**   We drove on a *bumpy* road.

The spelling of some words changes before you add -*y*.

> sun
> sun**ny**   It is a *sunny* day.

If a word ends with consonant, vowel, consonant, double the last consonant and add **-y** to form the adjective.

- Make each word an adjective.

  rain   mud   dust

- Read each sentence. Find the adjective.

  We played indoors on that rainy afternoon.
  The baby stepped in the muddy water.
  I wiped the dusty table.

Talk About It

Make the word that comes after each sentence into an adjective. Use the adjective to complete the sentence.

1. I live on a ___ street. (hill)
2. This is a ___ beach. (sand)
3. We walked on a ___ path. (rock)
4. It is a ___ morning. (sun)

Skills Practice

Make the word in ( ) into an adjective.
Complete the sentence with the adjective.
Write the sentence.

1. We had ___ fish for dinner. (salt)
2. I washed the ___ dishes. (dirt)
3. I put my ___ hands in the water. (soap)
4. They wiped the ___ glasses. (spot)
5. The ___ dog barked. (hair)
6. The ___ girl made me laugh. (fun)
7. You have ___ shoes. (mud)
8. The ___ boy went to bed. (sleep)

Writing Sentences

Make each word an adjective. Then write two sentences to describe something. Use the adjectives in your sentences.

1. stick   **2.** fur

Sample Answer 1. We had salty fish for dinner.

Words That Sound the Same

When you write sentences, you need to spell words the right way. Sometimes two words sound the same. But they may not mean the same thing.

- Read these sentences out loud. How are the underlined words the same? How are they different?

I have a pet monkey.
The monkey has one blue eye.

Words like I and eye sound the same. They are not spelled the same. They do not have the same meaning.

- Read each pair of sentences. How are the underlined words the same? Spell each underlined word. Tell its meaning.

I see the ship.
The ship sails on the sea.

The water was blue.
The wind blew hard.

Do you know a sailor?
No, I never met one.

The sail was torn.
They took it to a sale.

Sailors write home often.
He was right about the storm.

Do you hear the wind?
It is calm here now.

The sailors have two ships.
They want to buy another one.
They have a rowboat, too.

Talk About It

Use the correct word in each sentence. Give a
reason for your answer.

1. I like the ___ dress. (blew, blue)
2. Did you ___ it? (see, sea)
3. It is on ___ in the store. (sail, sale)
4. I want ___ buy it. (two, to, too)

Skills Practice

Choose the word with the correct meaning for each
sentence. Write the sentence.

1. Do you ___ about the new pet store? (no, know)
2. It is near ___ . (hear, here)
3. The fish are on ___ . (sail, sale)
4. One fish has a green ___ . (eye, I)
5. They come from the deep ___ . (sea, see)
6. I have ___ money. (no, know)
7. Do you want ___ dollars? (two, to, too)
8. Can ___ buy the fish now? (eye, I)

Writing Sentences

Pretend you work in a library. Write a sentence
using each word.

1. two   **3.** to
2. blue   **4.** hear

Sample Answer **1.** Do you know about the new pet store?

Skills Review

Read each sentence. Write a synonym for the underlined word. The words in the box may help you.

large	tiny
pretty	friendly
noisy	wonderful

1. You like <u>loud</u> music.
2. I have a <u>big</u> box of records.
3. A <u>nice</u> girl gave them to me.
4. I play a <u>lovely</u> song.
5. It tells a <u>good</u> story.
6. The record has a <u>small</u> scratch.

Read each sentence. Write an antonym for the underlined word. The words in the box may help you.

clean	small
slow	wet
old	full
low	weak

7. We baked a <u>big</u> cake.
8. I used a <u>new</u> mix.
9. You washed the <u>empty</u> bowl.
10. You put the <u>dry</u> bowl away.
11. I washed the <u>dirty</u> sponge.
12. We are <u>fast</u> workers.
13. We used a <u>strong</u> pan.
14. It was on a <u>high</u> shelf.

Make the word in ( ) into an adjective. Complete the sentence with the adjective. Write the adjective.

15. I laughed at the ____ monkey.   (hair)

16. He made a ____ face.   (fun)

17. We went to a ____ beach.   (sand)

18. It was a ____ day.   (sun)

19. We drove on a ____ road.   (dust)

Choose the word with the correct meaning for each sentence. Write the word.

20. I have ____ gloves.   (to, two, too)

21. I wear them ____ keep warm.   (to, two, too)

22. I bought them on ____ .   (sail, sale)

23. The gloves are ____ .   (blew, blue)

24. The store has ____ more gloves.   (know, no)

25. Can ____ wear them tonight?   (I, eye)

Copy the words below on a sheet of paper. Draw a line from each word at the left to its antonym. The antonyms are listed at the right. The first one is done for you.

stop	late
early	hate
open	go
love	cry
laugh	shut

up

down

Exploring Language

Taking Notes

You often read books for a special reason. Sometimes you need to gather facts for a report.

It is hard to remember all the important facts after you finish reading. You can help yourself remember important facts by taking notes. When you *take notes,* you write down all the important facts.

Andy has to write a report about what a painter must do before she begins to paint. He read this paragraph.

A painter must do many things before she starts her work. First she decides what she wants to paint. She may want to paint a picture of some flowers. Then she must decide what colors she will use. The colors will add to her painting. Finally she gathers her paints and brushes together.

Andy took these notes as he read the paragraph.

1. A painter must do many things before she begins to paint.
2. She decides what she wants to paint.
3. She decides what colors she will use.
4. She gathers her paints and brushes together.

● Read Andy's notes again. All his notes tell what a painter must do before she begins painting. Notice that all his notes are complete sentences.

Talk About It

Read this paragraph.

> Dance is beautiful to watch. Dancers must train for many years. Many start when they are very young. Dancers must go to special schools. They spend a lot of time learning and practicing dance.

Pretend you have to write a report about training to be a dancer. Which of these notes would you take?

1. Dance is beautiful.
2. Dancers train for many years.
3. They go to special schools.
4. They spend much time learning and practicing dance.

Skills Practice

Read this paragraph.

> Pedro was going to be in a play. First he had to try out for a part. Then he had to learn the part. He and his sister went over it many times. Now everyone in the play has to practice together.

Pretend you have to write a report telling about Pedro's part in a play. Write the notes you would take.

1. Pedro had to try out for a part.
2. He had to learn the part.
3. His sister helped him learn his part.
4. Everyone in the play has to practice together.

Organizing Notes

When you give a report, you want to make sure everyone understands your ideas. You must put your facts in an order that makes sense. First you read to find the important facts. Then you take notes. Read your notes carefully.

● Look at Jane's notes.

> **1.** Many forests catch on fire every year.
> **2.** People cause most forest fires.
> **3.** Dry summers can cause some forest fires, too.
> **4.** Special fire fighters put out forest fires.

Jane's notes are in a good order. She numbered her notes in the order she will write them in her report. She will use her first note for her main idea sentence. She will use the other notes for her detail sentences. The facts in her paragraph will have the same order as the facts in her notes.

Talk About It

Read these notes. Put them in an order that makes sense.

1. It belongs to a family of stars.
2. The sun is really a star.
3. We call this family the *Milky Way*.
4. There are many other families of stars.

Skills Practice

Read these notes. Write them in an order that makes sense.

1. It started out as dust and hot gas.
2. The earth is very old.
3. The dust and gas were left over from the sun.
4. At last it began to look like it does now.
5. Slowly the earth changed.

Write these notes in an order that makes sense.

1. At first people tried to copy birds.
2. At last someone made an airplane.
3. People always wanted to fly.
4. Next people tried to copy kites.

Stories

Do you like to hear and to read stories? You can read stories in books. You can watch them on TV. In a good story you want to know what happened. You cannot stop reading or listening until you find out.

Most stories have three parts. The parts are called the *beginning*, the *middle*, and the *end*. The beginning of the story uses sentences that tell who or what the story is about. Some sentences also tell when and where the story happens. The sentences in the middle tell what happened to people or things in the story. The sentences in the end tell how everything works out in the story.

- Read this story about a girl named Judy.

> Judy was sleeping one night. She heard strange noises downstairs. They sounded like someone was knocking things over. Judy was very scared. She woke her parents. Her mother called the police. Everyone looked around the house. To their surprise, they found the noise was made by Judy's dog. He was playing with his bone.

The story about Judy has a beginning, a middle, and an end. The beginning tells that the story is about Judy. It also tells when and where the story happened. The middle tells the problem that Judy had. The end tells how the problem was solved.

Talking About Stories

Read the story on the other page.

1. Which sentences tell what happened at the beginning of the story?

2. Which sentences tell what happened in the middle of the story?

3. Which sentences tell what happened at the end of the story?

4. Think of another ending for the story. What would it be?

A Class Story

Thinking About Stories

Your class is going to write a story together. Your story should have a beginning, a middle, and an end. Your story will be about a spaceship that lands outside your school. The picture below may help you think of sentences to write for each part of your story. Talk about what you want to happen in the beginning and middle of your story. How will your story end?

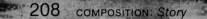

Writing a Story

Your teacher will write the story on the board.

1. You may begin your story with these two sentences: *One morning we were sitting in class. Suddenly we heard a loud noise outside.*

2. Now you are ready to write the middle of your story. Think of one or two sentences that describe the spaceship that landed. Think of one or two sentences that tell about the space people who step out.

3. Reread the middle part. Did you choose adjectives that really help you see the spaceship and the space people?

4. Now write the end of your story. Think of one or two sentences that tell what happened to the space people and the spaceship. You might tell what your class did.

5. Reread your whole story together. Does it have an interesting middle and end? You may want to write the story and draw your own pictures to go with it.

...icing a Story

Thinking About a Story

You are now going to write a story. Think of your own ideas or use the following ideas for your story. Remember your story must have a beginning, a middle, and an end.

Imagine that a person named Ray went to the zoo. Look at the pictures. What happened to Ray? Use the Word Bank to help write your story.

Word Bank

red
cap
visited
fed
peanuts
grabbed
yelled
zookeeper
laughed
funny

Writing Your Story

1. Begin your story with these two sentences. *Ray went to the zoo. He visited the monkeys.*
2. Write the middle of your story. Look at the pictures. Write one or two sentences that tell what Ray did when he visited the monkeys. Then write one or two sentences that tell what the monkey did with Ray's cap.
3. Write the end of your story. Did Ray get his cap back? How did he get it back? Write one or two sentences for the end of your story.

Edit Your Story

Read your story carefully. Answer these questions.

1. Does your story have a beginning, a middle, and an end?
2. Do your sentences tell clearly what happened in each part of the story?
3. What adjectives did you use in your sentences?
4. Did you use capital letters and periods where they are needed? Did you indent the first word?
5. Did you spell the words correctly? Use the Word Bank to help you.

Correct your mistakes. If you need to, write your story again. You may want to read your story to the class.

Editing Symbols

≡	make a capital letter
¶	indent
✄	take out
∧	add

INDEPENDENT WRITING
A Story

Prewriting Fairy tales are imaginary stories. Imagine you are walking in a park. You save a kitten from a big dog. To your surprise the kitten speaks to you. It promises you three wishes. Think about your wishes. What will happen to you as each wish comes true? Jot down notes or ideas you will use in the beginning, middle, and end of your story.

Writing Write a fairy tale about your three wishes. Use your notes to write the beginning, the middle, and the end of your story.

Editing Use the check questions and the editing symbols above to edit your story.

Unit Review

Write each adjective. Then write the noun it
describes. *pages 184-184*

1. Kevin has clean paper.

2. He found a red pen.

3. He drew a little clown.

4. The clown had big ears.

Write an adjective to complete each sentence. *pages 186-187*

5. The ___ snow fell fast.

6. She wore ___ mittens.

7. I made a ___ snowball.

8. He drank some ___ milk.

Write the correct adjective to fill each blank. *pages 188-189*

9. Joe wore a warm hat.
   Judy wore a ___ hat than Joe's.   (warmest, warmer)

10. Ellie wore the ___ hat of all.   (warmest, warmer)

Write a number word to complete each sentence. *page 190*

11. I have ___ stamps.

12. I buy ___ book.

13. Kim owns ___ coins.

14. She finds ___ jars.

Complete each sentence. Write the article. *page 191*

15. Tim flies ___ airplane.

16. It is only ___ toy.

17. Tim went to ___ airport.

18. He saw ___ real airplane.

Write a synonym for the underlined word. *page 194*

large	good	shiny	lovely

19. Cathy made a <u>pretty</u> bowl.

20. She used <u>bright</u> colors.

21. I found some <u>big</u> flowers.

22. A <u>nice</u> woman bought it.

Write an antonym for the underlined word. *page 195*

big	closed	bottom	dry

23. I saw an <u>open</u> door.   **25.** He sat on the <u>top</u> step.

24. A <u>little</u> boy ran out.   **26.** The boy had a <u>wet</u> towel.

Write the word with the correct meaning for each sentence.

pages 198-199

27. My school is near ____.   (here, hear)

28. I have gone there for ____ years.   (to, two, too)

Read these sentences from a story. Think about the right order for the sentences. *pages 206-211*

29. a. He was afraid to come down.

    b. She called the fire station.

    c. One morning Mops ran up a tall tree.

    d. Angela owned a pet monkey named Mops.

    e. A fire fighter climbed up and saved Mops.

    f. Angela could not reach him.

    g. Mops liked to climb trees.

Now put the sentences in order.

30. First, write the sentences that tell who, when, and where at the beginning of the story.

31. Next, write the sentences that tell about the problem in the middle of the story.

32. Last, write the sentences that tell how the problem was solved at the end of the story.

Have you ever thought of exploring a new place? Suppose you got lost along the way. What would you do? In this story, a young boy and his pony travel along an old trail. Follow the characters and share their adventure with them.

Blaze Finds the Trail

One day Billy's mother made some sandwiches for him, because he and Blaze were going for a very long ride. They were going to explore an old road through the woods that no one ever used any more. This was exciting. Blaze seemed to enjoy the ride as much as Billy.

They came to the place where the old road turned off, straight into the deep woods. Although it was overgrown with grass and weeds, Billy could still see the deep ruts wagons had made in the ground many years ago. He wanted to see where they would take them.

They came to a place where a dead tree was leaning across the road. There was barely room for Blaze to go under it. Billy had to lie flat on Blaze's back, and they just squeezed through.

Then they came to a fallen tree across the road, but Blaze was a fine jumper and sailed over it easily.

They had gone a long way, when Billy saw another big tree across the path. The branches held it up, so that it was too high to jump and too low to go under. Billy hated to turn back when they had come so far.

"Let's try to go around it, Blaze," said Billy. "There must be some way to do it."

The woods were very thick, and each time they tried to get back to the path there were fallen trees or thick woods in the way. They were getting farther and farther from the old road, and still they could not find any opening.

At last they were able to turn back toward the road. Now Billy felt that everything was going to be all right. But they had not gone far before they came to a very deep gully. Billy's heart sank, for he knew they could never get down such a place. They would have to go back again and try a different way. Billy had to lead his pony, for the woods were too thick for him to ride.

There was nothing in sight but woods, and Billy began to be worried. Which way was the road? When he looked for the sun to find what direction he should go, he saw that the sky had become very dark and stormy. It looked very strange, and he was frightened. They must get home before the storm.

It was growing very dark and still they could find no sign of a road. Billy was tired and frightened. He knew they were lost. He sat down to rest. Blaze rubbed his soft nose against Billy as if to say, "Don't worry, I'll take care of you." But now a strong wind was blowing, and the sky was very dark.

When Billy got up, Blaze started off pulling Billy with him. He seemed to know just where he wanted to go, so Billy followed him.

"Do you really know the way, Blaze?" he cried. "If you only get us out of these woods, I'll give you carrots and sugar every day. Lots and lots of them."

Blaze went right on, dodging around rocks and trees, but always going the same direction.

Suddenly, through the bushes, Billy saw something that made him very happy. It was only an old stone wall, but now he knew they were on the right track. His father had often told how the early settlers had built these walls, with stones they cleared from the land. And where there were walls, there had once been fields and roads leading to them.

Then just ahead he saw an opening in the wall, and a path leading ahead.

"You are wonderful, Blaze!" he cried. "You've found the way."

Now at last he could get in the saddle again, and they could go faster. The wind was growing stronger, and he knew the woods were no place to be in a storm.

They went at a gallop, for the wind was roaring through the treetops and the sky was very black. Suddenly they heard a loud crack, and Blaze leaped forward just as a big dead tree crashed down in the path behind them. "This must be another hurricane." Billy shouted to Blaze. "We'll have to race."

Blaze was galloping as hard as he could, and Billy was dodging the low branches when he saw, just ahead of them, a wide road. Nothing had ever looked so wonderful to him. Now he knew that home was just a mile down the road.

"You did it!" Billy shouted in Blaze's ear as the wind howled around them. "You're a wonderful pony!"

— *C. W. Anderson*

Creative Activities

1. **Creative Writing** Open any book and look on the page until you find the name of a person, such as "doctor." Then look for the name of a place, such as "field." Then find the name of an object, such as "tire." Write a story involving the three words you have selected. For example, your story might tell about a doctor with a tire in a field. Think of some problem that the person must solve in the story.

2. Look in the library for other books about Blaze and Billy by C. W. Anderson. Read them and share the adventures with your class.

SOCCER PLAYER

Grammar and Related Language Skills

Review of Verbs in the Present and Past
Verbs in the Future
Helping Verbs
Adverbs
Contractions

Practical Communication

STUDY AND REFERENCE SKILLS
Using the Library
COMPOSITION
Writing a Report

Creative Expression

A True Story

Do you like sports? People who report sports events on radio or television are called sports announcers. They must describe and explain the events clearly. What listening and speaking skills must a sports announcer have? People who report sports in newspapers or magazines are called sports reporters. What writing skills must they have?

219

Verbs in the Present and Past

Verbs are very important words in sentences. A *verb* is a word that names an action. It is in the predicate part of a sentence. The *predicate part* of a sentence tells what action the subject part does. Words like *run, jump,* and *climb* are verbs.

Ted <u>buys</u> a fishing pole.   Shelly <u>finds</u> a sleeping bag.

Verbs name actions. They also tell when the action happens. When you talk about things that happen now, you use a *verb in the present.*

A **verb in the present** names an action that happens now.

When you talk about things that happened before, you use a *verb in the past.*

A **verb in the past** names an action that happened before.
Mr. Peck <u>talked</u> to our class.
He <u>showed</u> us some maps.

Add **-s** to most verbs in the present when they work with singular nouns.
Jane <u>swims</u> in the pool.

If a verb ends in **s, ss, ch, sh,** or **x,** add **-es** to make the verb work with a singular noun.
Mr. Peck <u>teaches</u> school.

Talk About It

Use the correct verb in the present.

1. Helen ____ to school.   (rush)
2. The children ____ in the yard.   (play)
3. Mike ____ his friend.   (see)

Use the correct verb in the past.

4. Susan ____ unusual stamps.   (save)
5. She ____ the stamps in a book.   (place)
6. Her sister ____ the book to school.   (carry)
7. I ____ the stamps yesterday.   (study)

Skills Practice

Use the correct verb in the present. Write the sentence.

1. Chris ____ a model sailboat.   (build)
2. She ____ for strong wood.   (search)
3. Tod ____ the new sailboat in the lake.   (try)
4. He ____ the broken sail.   (fix)
5. They ____ the sailboat in a race.   (enter)

Use the correct verb in the past. Write the sentence.

6. I ____ in the woods last week.   (walk)
7. We ____ along the trails.   (move)
8. Barbara ____ the tent.   (carry)
9. Uncle Ray ____ in the lake.   (fish)
10. Tommy ____ the eggs.   (fry)
11. He ____ the new frying pan.   (try)

Sample Answers **1.** Chris builds a model sailboat. **6.** I walked in the woods last week.

Verbs in the Future

You know that verbs can tell about things that happen now. Verbs can tell about things that already happened. Verbs can also tell about things that will happen in the future.

- Look at the verbs in these sentences.

  Luis <u>swims</u> in the pool.   He <u>learned</u> to dive yesterday.

  The verb *swims* names an action that happens in the present time. The verb *learned* names an action that happened in the past.

- Now read this sentence.

  Luis <u>will swim</u> in a race next week.   He <u>will try</u> to win.

  The verbs *will swim* and *will try* name actions that will happen at a future time.

    The **future tense of a verb** names an action that will take place in the future.

  Verbs that show action in the future have a main verb and the helping verb *will* or *shall*.

    A **helping verb** is a verb that helps the main verb to name an action.

Talk About It

Find the verb in each sentence. Tell whether the
verb names an action in the present, the past, or
the future.

1. Linda Campos will swim in the race next Tuesday.
2. Her sister raced on our team last week.
3. The whole Campos family likes sports.
4. Mr. Campos will watch the races all day.
5. Mrs. Campos swims on a team also.
6. She liked the water when she was very young.

Skills Practice

Write each verb. Then write whether each verb is
in the **present**, the **past**, or the **future**.

1. Tommy O'Brien plays baseball.
2. He played baseball with his team this morning.
3. They will play again tomorrow morning.
4. Our town will have another baseball team soon.
5. Their shirts will be red.
6. I like football better than baseball.
7. My father watched my game last week.
8. He yelled very loudly.
9. My team uses the school football field.
10. We want to win all our games.

Sample Answer 1. plays, present

Using Verbs in the Past

You know that a verb in the past names an action that happened before. You add -ed to most verbs to name an action in the past. Some verbs do not follow the usual rule. Sometimes the whole word changes.

Here are some verbs that change to name an action in the past.

VERB	VERB IN THE PAST
go	went
see	saw
do	did
eat	ate
know	knew
fly	flew
give	gave
grow	grew
take	took
begin	began

- Read each sentence. Notice the verb that names an action in the past.

We <u>went</u> to the game.
A player <u>saw</u> the ball.
Our team <u>did</u> very well.
We <u>ate</u> some peanuts.
We <u>knew</u> many people

The ball <u>flew</u> up high.
We all <u>gave</u> a cheer.
Our hopes <u>grew</u> higher.
One player <u>took</u> his turn.
The band <u>began</u> to play.

Talk About It

Complete each sentence. Use a verb that names an action in the past.

1. Our class ___ to the race.   (go)
2. A girl ___ the finish line.   (see)
3. What ___ she do?   (do)
4. We ___ hot dogs after the race.   (eat)

Skills Practice

Read each sentence. Write each sentence with the verb that names an action in the past.

1. I ___ to the park.   (go)
2. Many trees ___ there.   (grow)
3. A boy ___ an apple to his friend.   (give)
4. He ___ a handstand.   (do)
5. He ___ he would fall.   (know)
6. Two girls ___ turns swinging.   (take)
7. Two birds ___ from the tree.   (fly)
8. A boy ___ a race.   (begin)

Writing Sentences

Pretend your class took a trip yesterday.

1. Write a sentence to tell where you *went.*
2. Write a sentence to tell what you *saw.*
3. Write a sentence to tell what you *did.*

Sample Answer 1. I went to the park.

Helping Verbs

Sometimes verbs need help to name an action in the past. The words *have* and *has* can be helping verbs.

- Read these sentences.

> Barbara <u>has</u> <u>played</u> well with our team.
> We <u>have</u> <u>practiced</u> all day.

The words *has* and *have* help the verbs to name an action.

> A **helping verb** is a word that helps a verb to name an action.

- Look at the sentences in the box again. When you use a helping verb with a verb, the form of the verb changes.

> Add **-ed** to most verbs when you use them with the helping verb *have* or *has.*

- Read each sentence. What is the verb? What is the helping verb?

The game has started.
She has jumped very high.
They have scored two points.
The players have walked out of the gym.

Talk About It

Complete each sentence with the correct form of the verb.

1. Bob has ＿＿ the game. (start)
2. Sue has ＿＿ the ball. (kick)
3. They have ＿＿ for a long time. (play)
4. We have ＿＿ the team. (join)
5. Cory has ＿＿ to first base. (walk)

Skills Practice

Read each sentence. Write the helping verb and the verb.

1. Mindy has wanted a new ball.
2. She has earned some money.
3. I have listed our names.
4. We have started a new game.

Write each sentence using the correct form of the verb.

5. We have ＿＿ tennis everyday. (play)
6. Ted has ＿＿ a lot. (learn)
7. He has ＿＿ me for my help. (thank)
8. I have ＿＿ the games. (enjoy)
9. Jane has ＿＿ to our town. (move)
10. She has ＿＿ schools. (change)
11. We have ＿＿ to her. (talk)
12. She has ＿＿ basketball. (play)
13. We have ＿＿ a good player. (need)

Sample Answers 1. has wanted **5.** We have played tennis everyday.

More Verbs in the Past

Remember that some verbs do not add -ed to name an action in the past. The verbs go, see, do, and eat change completely. These verbs change again when they are used with have or has.

VERB	PAST WITH HAVE OR HAS
go	have or has gone
see	have or has seen
do	have or has done
eat	have or has eaten
know	have or has known
fly	have or has flown
give	have or has given
grow	have or has grown
take	have or has taken
begin	have or has begun

• Read each sentence. Find the verb and helping verb.

My sister has gone out.   She has flown to the city.
I have seen her run.   We have given her a prize.
She has done her best.   Her score has grown.
She has eaten well.   She has taken first place.
We have known for a week.   Her race has begun.

Talk About It

Tell the correct form of the verb.

1. Some children have ___ to the barn.   (go)
2. They have ___ a lot of work there.   (do)
3. A girl has ___ a little pony.   (see)
4. The pony has ___ some hay.   (eat)

Skills Practice

Read each sentence. Write the helping verb and the verb.

1. We have gone to a race.
2. I have seen the winner.
3. She has done a good job.
4. He has eaten a good meal.

Write each sentence using the correct form of the verb.

5. Pat has ___ what he had to do.   (know)
6. He has ___ through his work.   (fly)
7. The children have ___ him their help.   (give)
8. Pat's score has ___ higher.   (grow)
9. We have ___ a picnic lunch to the game.   (take)
10. It has ___ to rain.   (begin)

Writing Sentences

Pretend you have gone to a ball game.

1. Write a sentence to tell where you *have gone*.
2. Write a sentence to tell what you *have seen*.
3. Write a sentence to tell what you *have done* there.

Sample Answers 1. have gone 5. Pat has known what he had to do.

Skills Review

Use the correct verb in the present. Write the verb.

1. A bird ___ for food.   (search)
2. It ___ through the clouds.   (fly)
3. The bird ___ insects in the grass.   (catch)

Use the correct verb in the past. Write the verb.

4. The cat ___ up a tree.   (race)
5. Sally ___ everywhere.   (look)
6. The baby ___ about the lost cat.   (cry)

Write each verb. Then write whether the verb is in the **present,** the **past,** or the **future.**

7. The cat slept.   9. The bird sings loudly.
8. The dog will bark.   10. Pilar will laugh.

Write the verb that names an action in the past.

11. He ___ to the football game.   (go)
12. We ___ two boxes of popcorn.   (eat)
13. She ___ the touchdown.   (see)

Write the helping verb and the verb.

14. You have played tennis.   16. She has raced ahead.
15. He has practiced hard.   17. I have tossed the ball.

Write the correct form of the verb.

18. Diane has ___ the most points.   (score)
19. Mike has ___ the highest.   (jump)
20. They have ___ very well.   (play)
21. We have ___ in first place.   (finish)

Write the helping verb and the verb.

22. I have gone to the schoolyard.
23. She has eaten lunch.
24. We have done this every afternoon.
25. He has seen them often.

Write the correct form of the verb.

26. She has ___ a new fishing rod for Tim.   (see)
27. We have ___ to buy it.   (go)
28. Tim has ___ us to the store.   (take)
29. He has ___ dinner with us.   (eat)
30. Sue has ___ her model airplane.   (fly)
31. She has ___ to build model airplanes.   (begin)

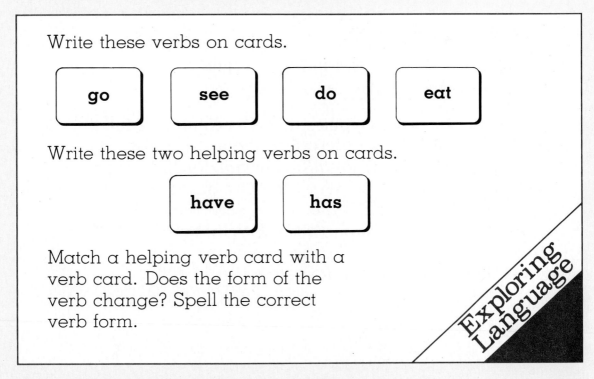

Write these verbs on cards.

| go | see | do | eat |

Write these two helping verbs on cards.

| have | has |

Match a helping verb card with a verb card. Does the form of the verb change? Spell the correct verb form.

Exploring Language

Adverbs

You have learned that a verb names an action. Other words in a sentence describe an action. These words tell more about an action.

- Read this sentence.

Pedro pulled the wagon <u>quickly</u>

The word *quickly* is an adverb. It tells about the verb *pushed*. It tells *how* Pedro pushed.

> An **adverb** is a word that describes an action.

Sometimes you will find adverbs near the beginning of a sentence. At other times you will find adverbs near the end of a sentence.

- Read these sentences.

<u>Carefully</u> Nick hopped into the wagon.
Pedro waved <u>happily</u>.

The word *carefully* comes at the beginning of the first sentence. But it describes the action verb *hopped*. The word *carefully* tells *how* Nick hopped. The word *happily* comes at the end of the second sentence. It describes the action verb *waved*. The word *happily* tells *how* Pedro waved. Both *carefully* and *happily* are adverbs. They each tell about an action. They each tell *how* an action is done.

Talk About It

What is the adverb in each sentence? What verb
does it describe?

1. Eagerly I rowed the boat.
2. The sun shone brightly.
3. Calmly I checked the water.
4. Slowly a turtle swam near me.
5. I turned the boat carefully.
6. A duck watched quietly.

Skills Practice

Write each sentence. Underline the adverb in each
sentence. Then write the verb it describes.

1. A crow called angrily.
2. Softly I whistled.
3. Fish jumped lazily.
4. Rapidly I pulled.
5. A frog croaked cheerfully.
6. Happily I grinned at it.
7. A breeze blew lightly.
8. Loudly Pedro called.
9. Sadly I turned the boat.
10. I reached shore quickly.
11. Hungrily we ate lunch.
12. Clouds formed quickly.
13. Rain fell suddenly.
14. We ran excitedly.
15. Cheerfully we waited.
16. Pedro sang merrily.
17. Gladly I joined him.
18. Slowly the rain stopped.
19. Birds sang sweetly.
20. Quietly we listened.

Sample Answer 1. A crow called *angrily.* called

More Adverbs

An adverb is a word that describes an action. You already know that some adverbs tell *how* an action is done. Other adverbs can tell *when* an action is done.

● Read these sentences.

Mia raced <u>today</u>.   <u>First</u> she exercised.

The word *today* is an adverb. It tells *when* Mia raced. The word *first* is also an adverb. It tells when Mia *exercised*. Notice that *today* comes at the end of the sentence. The adverb *first* comes at the beginning of the sentence. Sometimes adverbs that tell *when* appear at the beginning of a sentence. Other times adverbs that tell *when* appear at the end of a sentence.

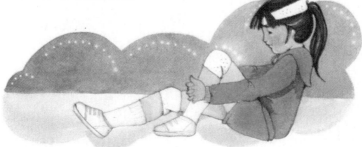

● Read these sentences.

Mia swam <u>next</u>.   <u>Then</u> she rested.

In the first sentence, *next* describes the action verb *swam*. The word *next* tells *when* Mia swam. In the second sentence, *then* describes the action verb *rested*. The word *then* tells *when* Mia rested. The words *next* and *then* are adverbs. They tell *when* the action is done.

Talk About It

What is the adverb in each sentence?

1. Todd went to the park today.
2. First he climbed some trees.
3. Then his friends jumped rope.
4. They all played ball next.
5. Now they rest on the swings.

Skills Practice

Write each sentence. Draw a line under the adverb in each sentence. Then draw two lines under the verb each adverb describes.

1. Yesterday we visited the shore.
2. My family goes often.
3. We arrived early.
4. First we unpacked the car.
5. We reached the beach next.
6. Soon the sun warmed us.
7. Then we all swam.
8. Our friends joined us later.
9. We ate lunch last.
10. Finally we rested.

Writing Sentences

Think about a special place to play. Write four sentences about it. In the first two sentences, use adverbs telling *how* an action is done. In the next two sentences, use adverbs telling *when* an action is done.

Sample Answer 1. <u>Yesterday</u> we <u>visited</u> the shore.

Contractions

Sometimes you use short cuts when you write. Some words can be joined together to make a shorter word that means the same thing.

can not	do not	does not
can't	don't	doesn't
did not	have not	has not
didn't	haven't	hasn't

A **contraction** is a word made up of two words. The words are joined together to make one word. One or more letters are left out.

Use an **apostrophe** (') in a contraction to take the place of the letter or letters that are left out.

● Read each pair of sentences. Find the contraction. What words make up each contraction?

I can not swim very well.
I can't swim very well.

I did not bring my bathing suit.
I didn't bring my bathing suit.

He does not own a boat.
He doesn't own a boat.

We have not found the lake.
We haven't found the lake.

Talk About It

Read each sentence using a contraction for the underlined words. Spell the contraction.

1. Our player <u>does not</u> have the ball.
2. He <u>has not</u> scored a point.
3. We <u>can not</u> stop the other team.
4. Our fans <u>do not</u> look happy.
5. We <u>have not</u> lost yet.
6. They <u>did not</u> blow the whistle.

Skills Practice

Write each sentence using a contraction for the underlined words.

1. Max <u>can not</u> catch the ball.
2. Molly <u>does not</u> have a glove.
3. The team <u>has not</u> found a coach.
4. My friends <u>have not</u> come.
5. They <u>do not</u> like basketball.
6. We <u>did not</u> play well.
7. We <u>can not</u> find an empty space.

Writing Sentences

Write a sentence about each of these. Use a contraction.

1. Something you can not do
2. Something you do not like to do

Sample Answer 1. Max can't catch the ball.

Prefixes

Some words are formed by adding a letter or letters to the beginning of other words.

A **prefix** is a group of letters added to the beginning of a word.

The prefix *un-* can mean *the opposite of.*

Barry <u>hooked</u> the gate.

A visitor <u>unhooked</u> it.

We <u>lock</u> the door each night.

We <u>unlock</u> it in the morning.

The prefix *re-* often means *again.*

Ms. Parker <u>filled</u> her plate.   Mr. Kane <u>built</u> a doghouse.
Later she <u>refilled</u> it.   He <u>rebuilt</u> it a year later.

• Read each pair of sentences.

Joan tied her shoes.   Larry read the story.
She untied them at bedtime.   He reread it for his friend.

Look at the verbs. What prefix was added in the second sentence of each pair? How does the prefix change the meaning of the verb?

Talk About It

Add the prefix *un-* to each verb to make a new verb. What does the new verb mean?

1. cover   **2.** snap   **3.** do

Add the prefix *re-* to each verb to make a new verb. What does the new verb mean?

4. paint   **5.** write   **6.** visit

Skills Practice

Add the prefix *un-* to each underlined verb. Write the second sentence with the new verb.

1. Brady <u>buttons</u> his coat.
   He _____ it on warm days.

2. Bea <u>snapped</u> her boots.
   One boot came _____ .

3. I <u>zip</u> my coat outdoors.
   I _____ it indoors.

4. We <u>packed</u> the box.
   They _____ it.

Add the prefix *re-* to each underlined verb. Write the second sentence with the new verb.

5. Mother <u>told</u> a story.
   She _____ it many times.

6. Father <u>opened</u> the door.
   He _____ it for my sister.

7. I <u>packed</u> a bag.
   I _____ it at the motel.

8. Alice <u>played</u> the record.
   She _____ it later.

Writing Sentences

Write one sentence using each of the following verbs: *untie, unlock, reopen, reshovel.*

Sample Answers **1.** He unbuttons it on warm days. **5.** She retold it many times.

Different Ways to Say Something

You talk to your friends in certain ways. You often use different words when you talk to your teacher.

• Read the sentence below each picture.

Hey Jack!

Excuse me, Mrs. Walters.

In the first picture the children are talking to each other. They use everyday words. In the second picture the student is speaking to an adult. She is choosing her words more carefully.

You also write things in different ways at different times. You choose everyday words when you write to your friends. You choose words more carefully when you write to adults.

Dear Ted,
 What happened to you? Why weren't you at practice today? I hope you're okay.
 See you soon.
 Alan

Dear Mr. White,
 I am sorry to hear that you are ill. I hope that you will be feeling well enough to return to practice soon.
 Alan Smith

In the first note Alan wrote to his friend. He used everyday words. In the second note Alan wrote to an adult. He chose his words more carefully.

Talk About It

Pretend that you want to buy something in a store. Which group of words would you say to the store owner?

1. This is a neat bike.
   I like this bike very much.

2. This one is far out, too.
   I really like this one, too.

3. Look at this one.
   Get a load of this!

4. I'll give you a buzz when I've decided.
   I'll give you a call when I've decided.

5. Thank you very much.
   Thanks a bunch.

Pretend you are talking to the team coach in your school. Which group of words would you say?

6. I'm nuts about basketball.
   I enjoy basketball a lot.

7. I can run like crazy.
   I can run very fast.

8. How come I can't join the team?
   Why can't I join the team?

9. I understand.
   I got it.

Skills Review

Write each sentences. Draw a line under the adverb in each sentence. Then draw two lines under the verb each adverb describes.

1. Yesterday we went camping.
2. George and I walked slowly.
3. Suddenly a deer appeared.
4. We watched the deer quietly.
5. Then the deer noticed us.
6. It ran off quickly.

Read each sentence using a contraction. Write the contraction.

7. I do not fish very often.
8. He has not brought enough worms.
9. We can not find the new hooks.
10. They did not know about the lake.
11. She does not have a fishing rod.
12. We have not caught any fish.

Read the first sentence in each pair. Add the prefix *un-* to the underlined verb. Write the new verb that will complete the second sentence.

13. He <u>covers</u> the bird cage at night.
    He ____ it in the morning.

14. I always <u>lock</u> the car door.
    I will ____ it now.

15. The woman <u>tied</u> my packages together.
    I ____ them when I got home.

16. Fay <u>wrapped</u> a gift for Pedro.
Pedro ____ it at his birthday party.

Read the first sentence in each pair. Add the prefix
re- to the underlined verb. Write the new verb that
will complete the second sentence.

17. We <u>painted</u> the house two years ago.
Father ____ it this year.

18. I <u>wrote</u> a story.
I ____ it on clean paper.

19. She <u>packed</u> her suitcase.
She ____ it after her trip.

20. He <u>counted</u> the number of children on the bus.
He ____ when the children got off the bus.

People usually use contractions
when they talk to each other. A
contraction takes less time to say than
the two words that make up the
contraction.

Listen to two friends talking to
each other. Make a list of the
contractions they use. Next to each
word, write the two words that make
up the contractions.

Exploring Language

Dictionary: Words with Two Meanings

You can use a dictionary to find out what a word means. Sometimes a word can have two meanings. Then the dictionary tells both meanings. You will find **1.** in front of the first meaning. You will find **2.** in front of the second meaning.

- Look at this dictionary page. Find the word *draw*. What are the two meanings of *draw*?

---

dance/dust

dance **1.** To move the feet or body in time to music. Do you like to *dance*? **2.** A party where people dance. Susan and John are going to a *dance* tonight.

dart **1.** To move suddenly or quickly. The fox *darted* into the bushes. **2.** Something thin and pointed that looks like a small arrow.

date **1.** The day, month, year, or time when something happens. **2.** A sweet fruit that grows on a tree. Henry likes *dates* better than candy.

draw **1.** To make a picture of something. My teacher asked me to *draw* a picture of a balloon. **2.** To move something in a direction. The farmer used a donkey to *draw* her wagon.

dress **1.** To put on things to wear. Will you *dress* Carmen's new doll? **2.** Something girls and women wear. My mother bought me a *dress*.

dust **1.** Tiny pieces of earth or dirt. The rain cleared the *dust* from the air. **2.** To clean off something. Tony's brother will *dust* the tables.

- Read this sentence. Which meaning of *draw* fits this sentence?

The pony <u>draws</u> a small red cart.

Talk About It

Read each sentence. Use the sample dictionary page. Tell which meaning of *dart* fits each sentence.

1. They aimed the <u>darts</u> at the dart board.
2. The cat <u>darted</u> behind a fence.

Skills Practice

Look at the underlined word in each sentence. Use the sample dictionary page. Write **1.** if the word has the first meaning. Write **2.** if the word has the second meaning.

1. We made a bread out of <u>dates</u>.
2. The dolls <u>dance</u> on the music box.
3. I must <u>dust</u> all the old books.
4. What is the <u>date</u> of your birthday?
5. The <u>dust</u> made me sneeze.
6. I will <u>draw</u> a picture of the plane.
7. My best <u>dress</u> is too small now.

Sample Answer 1. 2.

Books of Information

Your school books tell you facts about many different things. Sometimes you need to find facts that you cannot find in your school books.

The library has books called reference books. *Reference books* give facts about many different subjects. They are very helpful when you do reports. The *dictionary* is a reference book. The *encyclopedia* and *atlas* are other reference books you can find in the library.

An *encyclopedia* is a set of books that gives facts about many things. The books are arranged in alphabetical order. You can find out about famous people. You can find information about different countries. You can learn about how people in other parts of the world live. Encyclopedias also give information about the latest discoveries in science. These are only some of the things you can find in an encyclopedia. It has information about almost everything.

An *atlas* is a book of maps. You can find maps of different countries in an atlas. Most atlases have an index to help you find the maps.

Talk About It

Name the reference book you would use to find out about each of these.

1. George Washington
2. A map of France
3. How the people in China live
4. The meaning of the word *humor*

Skills Practice

Name the reference book you would use to find out about each of these. Write **encyclopedia**, **dictionary**, or **atlas**.

1. The meaning of the word *cycle*
2. How skyscrapers are built
3. Christopher Columbus
4. A map of Mexico
5. The meaning of the word *orchard*
6. What makes an airplane fly
7. A map of the world
8. Early inventions
9. The meaning of the word *wizard*
10. How gold was discovered
11. A map of the United States
12. The history of baseball
13. The first trip to the moon

Sample Answer 1. dictionary

Doing a Survey

Very often you need to gather and organize information. A *survey* is a way of gathering and organizing information.

Matt wants to find out which sport the children in his class like best. He did this survey. He asked the children to choose either baseball, swimming, or skating. He wrote down each child's answer. Then he counted all the answers to see what sport most children picked. Last he made a graph to show the children's answers.

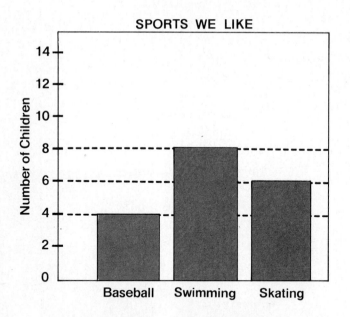

SPORTS WE LIKE

- Look at the graph.

It shows that four children like baseball. Eight children like swimming. Six children like skating. The children in the class like swimming the best.

- Notice how Matt did his survey.

He asked questions.
He wrote down the answers.
He counted all the different answers.
He made a graph to show the answers.

Talk About It

Rosa did a survey. The graph shows the information she gathered. Look at the graph. Which of these questions did Rosa ask?

1. Who has a dog for a pet?
2. Who has a cat for a pet?
3. Who has a bird for a pet?
4. Who has no pets?

Skills Practice

Stan did a survey. The graph shows the information he gathered. Look at the graph. Write a sentence to answer each of these questions.

1. How many children like bananas?

2. How many children like apples?

3. How many children like oranges?

4. Which fruit do the children like best?

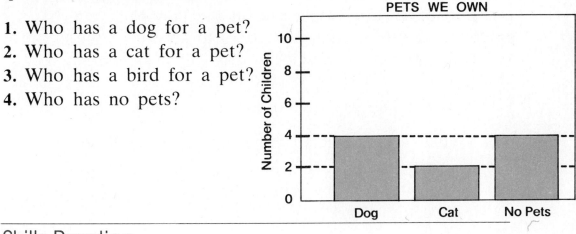

Sample Answer 1. Eight children like bananas.

Interviews and Reports

Thinking About Interviews and Reports

You have just won first place in a contest. You drew the best safety poster in your grade. There is going to be a story about you in the newspaper. A person from the newspaper comes to school to ask you some questions. The person is called a *reporter*.

● Look at the questions the reporter asks you.

> What is your name? How old are you? Who is your teacher? How did you get the idea for your poster? How long did it take you to make the poster?

The reporter used question words like *who, what, when, where, why,* and *how.* They help the reporter find out about you and the contest.

The reporter writes down all your answers. The questions and answers are called an *interview.* The reporter asks questions only about you and your poster. The reporter reads all the questions and answers in the interview very carefully. Then the reporter writes a report. The report tells about what you said.

Talking About Interviews and Reports

Paula wanted to write a report about playing soccer. She interviewed a player on the school soccer team. These are the questions Paula asked.

> How many players are on the soccer team? When does a team score points during a game? What are some of the rules in soccer?

Paula got these answers:

> There are eleven players on a soccer team. A team scores points when the ball is kicked past the goal line of the other team. Players cannot touch the ball with their hands or arms as they move down the field.

1. What is the first word in each question?
2. Why did Paula ask questions only about soccer?
3. What other questions could Paula ask?

Writing a Report

Pretend you want to write a report about being a school nurse. Write four questions you could ask your school nurse. Try to use question words like *who*, *what*, *why*, *where*, *when*, and *how*.

A Class Report

Your class is going to write a report together. Your report will be about Paula's soccer interview in the last lesson. You remember that Paula asked three questions about soccer. Here are the answers she got.

There are eleven players on a soccer team.
A team scores points when the ball is kicked past the goal line of the other team.
Players cannot touch the ball with their hands or arms as they move down the field.

Your report will use these answers. Your report should be one paragraph. You will need a main idea sentence. You can use the sentences above as your detail sentences.

Writing a Report

1. Your report will begin with a main idea sentence. Choose one of these sentences for the main idea sentence. Your teacher will write your report on the board.

Soccer is an interesting game to play.

There are many things to know about soccer.

2. Use Paula's first answer as the second sentence in your report.

3. Use Paula's second answer as the next sentence in your report.

4. Use Paula's third answer as the last sentence in your report.

5. Read your report. Does it tell some interesting things about soccer?

6. Write the finished report on your paper.

Careers

Do you like to read sports stories in newspapers and magazines? They are written by sports reporters. They interview sports stars and watch games. They must write interesting reports about them. Good sports reporters can write very well. They have good ideas and know how to write them. If you want to be a reporter, you must be a good writer.

Practicing a Report

Thinking About a Report

Now you will write a report. Pretend you interviewed a basketball player. You asked the person questions about the game last night. Here are the answers to your questions. They are not in the best order for your report.

They were very happy after the game.

Chris Mack scored in the last second.

Our team scored the first basket.

The other team had more points at half time.

Our team won the game.

Writing Your Report

1. Your report will be a paragraph. Begin your report with one of these main idea sentences.
   The basketball game last night was exciting.
   Everyone enjoyed the basketball game last night.
2. Look at the answers to the questions again. What is the best order of the sentences for your report? Write the sentences in that order. Your first sentences could be about which team scored first.

Edit Your Report

Read your report. Think about these questions.

1. Does your report tell about one main idea?
2. Did you use any helping verbs in your sentences? Which ones did you use?
3. Did you use capital letters and periods correctly? Did you indent the first sentence?

Correct your mistakes. If you need to, write your report again.

Editing Symbols

≡ make a capital letter

¶ indent

⤴ take out

∧ add

INDEPENDENT WRITING
A Feature Story Report

Prewriting   A feature story is a kind of report that describes a special person. You are going to write a feature story about a special person at your school. First you must choose a person. The person may be from your school.

   Then you must interview the person. First write the questions you want to ask the person. Remember that reporters use question words like *who, what, when, where,* and *why.* During the interview, note the person's answers to your questions. Reread your questions and answers.

Writing   Write a feature story about a special person in your school. Begin your feature story by telling the name and the job of the person you interviewed. Then write detail sentences that tell the person's answers to your questions.

Editing   Use the check questions and the editing symbols above to edit your feature story.

Unit Review

Write the correct form of the verb in the present. *pages 220–221*

1. Lisa ___ the table.   (clear)
2. Paul ___ the dishes.   (wash)
3. Betty ___ the glasses.   (dry)

Write the correct form of the verb in the past. *pages 220–221*

4. The children ___ to finish soon.   (hope)
5. Some friends ___ to play.   (wait)
6. Paul ___ the wagon.   (fix)

Write each verb. Then tell whether the verb is in the **present,** the **past,** or the **future.** *pages 222–223*

7. John bowls.
8. He will bowl on Saturday.
9. We bowled last week.
10. Our team will play soon.

Write the verb that names an action in the past. *pages 224–225*

11. Dora ___ breakfast early.   (eat)
12. I ___ to school on the bus.   (go)
13. You ___ our teacher.   (see)
14. We ___ our homework last night.   (do)

Write each sentence. Use the correct form of the verb. Underline the helping verb. *pages 226–227*

15. Mark has ___ the team.   (join)
16. John and Jim have ___ many times.   (play)
17. Gail has ___ the game.   (start)
18. A child has ___ the winner.   (pick)

Complete each sentence. Write the correct form of the verb. *pages 228–229*

19. The boy has ____ us home. (take)
20. He has ____ to the movies. (go)
21. The girl has ____ the same movie. (see)
22. They have ____ their jobs. (begin)

Write each sentence. Underline the adverb in each sentence. Then write the verb it describes. *pages 232–235*

23. Eagerly the two teams entered.
24. We cheered loudly.
25. Next the team captains shook hands.
26. Suddenly the whistle blew.
27. Then the game began.

Write the contraction for each pair of words. *pages 236–237*

28. can not   **29.** do not   **30.** did not
31. have not   **32.** does not   **33.** has not

You want to write a report about germs. You plan to interview the school nurse. Read these questions. Write the four questions that you should ask in the interview. *pages 246–249*

34. a. Where do germs come from?
  b. How do germs get in our bodies?
  c. What color is your office painted?
  d. When can germs do the most harm?
  e. Who are some famous people you have met?
  f. Why can't we see germs?

Many stories often tell about real people. This story was written by a girl from Hong Kong. Now she lives in the United States. She can write English very well. But she wants to keep speaking and writing Chinese, too. She knows that it is important to know another language. So she goes to two schools every day. Read about what she is learning in her Chinese school.

Chinese Brush Painting

My name is Wynne Lee, and I started to learn Chinese brush painting when I was six years old. It takes a long time to learn.

I learned Chinese and English in Hong Kong. I've been in the United States for four years. Here I go to an American school, and then every afternoon from 4:30 to 7 I go to a Chinese school.

I brought an ink box with me from Hong Kong, but you can buy

them in the United States. The box has cotton in it. You pour special writing ink into the box and you use a special brush.

Chinese is written from top to bottom and from left to right. Some Chinese words sound almost alike. Some look alike, too.

You hold the brush straight up. The real Chinese way is to write with the pen just under your nose, but most children don't do that. It's very hard.

Wynne Lee

Creative Activities

1. **Creative Writing** Wynne Lee knows how to write in two different ways. She can write the way you do. She can write in Chinese, too. You can write in two different ways, too. One way is with letters. Another is with your own pictures. Write a sentence that tells what you like to do when you have a vacation. On another piece of paper, draw a picture of what you like to do when you have a vacation.

2. Wynne Lee traveled a long way to get to the United States. She went from Hong Kong to Japan. Then she went to Hawaii. Finally she arrived in California. Use a class map. Use your finger to trace Wynne Lee's trip from Hong Kong to California.

SALZBURG MARIONETTES, AUSTRIA

Grammar and Related Language Skills

Review of Sentences
Nouns and Pronouns in Sentences
Verbs in Sentences
Building Sentences

Practical Communication

STUDY AND REFERENCE SKILLS
Learning About Facts and Opinions

COMPOSITION
Writing a Book Report

Creative Expression

A Story

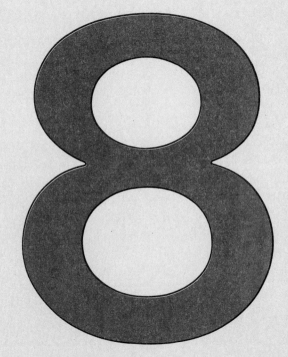

Have you ever seen or read a play? People who write plays are called playwrights. Playwrights write lines and scenes for their characters to perform. They also write the stage directions. What writing skills do playwrights need to create a play with characters and stage directions? What skills would you need to write an interesting play?

Reviewing Sentences

You have learned many things about sentences. A *sentence* is a group of words that states a complete idea. Some sentences tell something. Some sentences ask something. Some sentences show strong feeling.

A **telling sentence** is a sentence that tells something.

A **question sentence** is a sentence that asks something.

An **exclamation sentence** is a sentence that shows strong feeling.

- Read each sentence about the picture. Is it a telling sentence, a question sentence, or an exclamation sentence?

How beautiful the painting is!
A girl sits in the grass.
Do you see a house?
Who painted the picture?

When you write a sentence, you must begin and end it with special signs.

Use a **capital letter** to begin the first word of each sentence.

Use a **period** (.) at the end of a telling sentence.

Use a **question mark** (**?**) at the end
of a question sentence.

Use an **exclamation mark** (**!**) at the
end of an exclamation sentence.

Talk About It

Read each sentence. Is it a telling sentence, a
question sentence, or an exclamation sentence? What
special signs are missing?

1. I play the drums
2. the drum is broken

3. who broke it
4. What a good song that is

Skills Practice

Write each sentence correctly. Write **telling** if it is a
telling sentence. Write **question** if it is a question
sentence. Write **exclamation** if it is an exclamation
sentence.

   Have you read this story
2. a young girl grows up in the city.
3. her grandfather lives in the mountains
4. does she visit him
5. what a long trip it is
6. how happy she is

Writing Sentences

Think of a story you read. Write one telling sentence
about the story. Write one question sentence about
it. Write one exclamation sentence about it.

Sample Answer 1. Have you read this story? question

Nouns and Pronouns in the Subject Part

Every sentence has two parts. They work together to state a complete idea. The *subject part* of a sentence names whom or what the sentence is about. The *predicate part* of a sentence tells what action the subject part does.

● Look at this sentence. The blue part is the subject part. The red part is the predicate part.

Our class | put on a show.

Now you will take a closer look at the subject part of a sentence. Every subject has a noun or a pronoun. Words like *doctor, school,* and *car* are nouns. Words like *he, I,* and *they* are pronouns.

A **noun** is a word that names a person, a place, or a thing.

A **pronoun** is a word that takes the place of one or more nouns.

The subject part may have more than one word. The noun or pronoun is always the main word.

● Read each sentence. Look at the subject part. What is the main word in the subject part? Is it a noun or a pronoun?

The boy | played music.   Sandy | clapped.

He | blew a horn.   She | liked the song.

Talk About It

Read each sentence. What is the main word in the
subject part? Is it a noun or a pronoun?

1. Ron tripped. **3.** Two dancers helped.
2. He fell. **4.** They pulled Ron up.

Skills Practice

Write each sentence. Draw a line between the
subject part and the predicate part.

1. Pam goes to dancing school.
2. Jerry goes, too.
3. He jumps high in the air.
4. She moves across the floor quickly.
5. The children wear special clothes.
6. They practice everyday.

Read each sentence. Write the main word in the
subject part. Then write **noun** if the word is a noun.
Write **pronoun** if the word is a pronoun.

7. My mother took me to a show.
8. We saw many people.
9. A man told funny jokes.
10. He made us laugh.
11. A woman sang two songs.
12. Some people acted in a short play.
13. It made us laugh, too.
14. I had a good time.

Sample Answers **1.** Pam | goes to dancing school. **7.** mother, Noun

Verbs in Sentences

You have looked at the words in the subject part of a sentence. The main word in the subject part is a noun or a pronoun.

Now look at the predicate part. Remember, the *predicate part* of a sentence tells what action the subject part does. Every predicate part has a verb.

A **verb** is a word that names an action.

The predicate part may have more than one word. But the main word in the predicate part is the verb.

- Read each sentence. Look at the predicate part. What is the verb?

Susan | sang.

I | played the drums.

We | acted in a play, too.

Talk About It

Read each sentence. Find the verb.

1. Our class made costumes.
2. Anita cut the cloth.
3. Joe sewed with a needle.
4. Then we ironed them.

5. Maria sang a song.
6. Ted danced.
7. Jim clapped his hands.
8. They all laughed.

Skills Practice

Write each sentence. Underline the verb.

Roy draws a picture.
2. He paints carefully.
3. He colors a house red.
4. The picture hangs on the wall.
5. Peter writes stories.
6. He reads a story to the class.
7. They talk about the story.
8. Some children ask questions.
9. The class adds other sentences.
10. The teacher tells the class his ideas.

Writing Sentences

Pretend you saw a magic show. Write two sentences about the show. Use a noun in the subject part of one sentence. Use a pronoun in the subject part of the other sentence. Be sure to use a verb in each predicate part.

Sample Answer 1. Roy <u>draws</u> a picture.

Skills Review

Write each sentence correctly. Then write **telling** if it is a telling sentence. Write **question** if it is a question sentence. Write **exclamation** if it is an exclamation sentence.

1. my friends played records
2. what songs do they like
3. how beautifully they sing
4. Cathy hears the loud horn
5. Who listens to the piano
6. What a pretty song that is
7. Rose plays in a band
8. what a surprise that is
9. does Joe play music too
10. he takes dancing lessons

Read each sentence. Write the main word in the subject part. Then write **noun** if the word is a noun. Write **pronoun** if the word is a pronoun.

11. Karen plays the piano.
12. She practices every day.
13. John bakes bread.
14. He mixes the flour completely.
15. His mother adds the water.
16. They cook in the kitchen.
17. Lucy works with clay.
18. She shapes small figures.

19. They look like three elephants.
20. Their trunks curl up.
21. I made a birdhouse.
22. My sister helped.
23. We work well together.

Read each sentence. Write the verb.

24. My brother climbs mountains.
25. He jumps rope, too.
26. My sister skates every day.
27. She practices every morning.
28. They run many races.
29. Todd swims very well.
30. He joins a new team.
31. His team wins many prizes.
32. Beth plays softball.
33. She hits the ball hard.
34. The ball flies over a fence.
35. Everyone cheers for Beth.

Here is a puzzle. Make three sentences by using the correct circles.

(Pat) (.) (?) (D) (plane)

_____ flies the _____ . Can you paint _____
_____ ave likes apples _____

Exploring Language

Building Sentences

Every sentence you write must have a noun or a pronoun in the subject part. These words name whom or what the sentence is about.

	NOUN			PRONOUN	
SUBJECT PART	The girls	ran.	SUBJECT PART	We	watched.

You can make the subject part tell more. You can add words to the subject part to describe the noun. These words are adjectives.

An **adjective** is a word that describes a noun.

• Read these sentences.

The <u>two</u> girls ran.   The <u>happy</u> girls ran.

The adjectives *two* and *happy* were added to the subject part. They describe the noun *girls*. Each adjective tells you more about the noun *girls*.

Every sentence you write must have a verb in the predicate part. The verbs name the action the noun or pronoun does.

	VERB			VERB	
The girls	ran.	PREDICATE PART	We	watched.	PREDICATE PART

You can also make the predicate part tell more. You can add words to the predicate part to describe the action of the verb. These words are adverbs.

An **adverb** is a word that describes an action.

• Read these sentences.

The girls ran <u>quickly</u>.   The girls ran <u>yesterday</u>.

The adverbs *quickly* and *yesterday* were added to the predicate part. They describe the verb *ran*. Each adverb tells you more about how or when the girls *ran*.

Talk About It

Read each sentence. Add more words to the subject part to make a good sentence.

1. The boys played.
2. The girls laughed.
3. The dog barked.
4. The baby cried.

Read each sentence. Add more words to the predicate part to make a good sentence.

5. Tom called.
6. Jim answered.
7. They ran.
8. George followed.

Skills Practice

Add words to the subject part of each sentence. Then write the sentence.

1. The orchestra played.
2. The curtains opened.
3. The actors entered.
4. The audience clapped.
5. The child sang.
6. The boys danced.
7. The women laughed.
8. The men called.

Add words to the predicate part of each sentence. Then write the sentence.

1. The parade passes.
2. The drum major leads.
3. The band plays.
4. The players march.
5. The children follow.
6. The horns blast.
7. The whistle blows.
8. The crowd cheers.

Commas

When you speak, you use your voice to set apart certain words. When you write, you use *commas* to set apart certain words. Commas help your reader to understand your exact meaning.

Commas set apart words that break into a sentence. Sometimes you may begin a sentence with *yes, no,* or *well.* Other times you may begin or end a sentence with the name of a person who is spoken to directly.

> Use a **comma** (,) to set off words such as *yes, no,* and *well* when they begin a sentence.

Yes, I have two brothers.

> Use a **comma** (,) to set off the name of a person who is spoken to directly in a sentence.

Jane, please come here.   Did you hear me, Ari?

Commas also set apart the day of the month from the year.

> Use a **comma** (,) to separate the date from the year.

Rose wrote on March 3, 1982.

Commas set apart conversation words. Conversation words are words like *said, answered,* and *called.* They are words that tell how a person talked.

> Use a **comma** (,) after conversation words.

Meg said, "I lost my keys."   Roy called, "I see them."

Talk About It

Read each sentence. Tell how you would use commas.

1. Lee we must fix Mel's toy plane.
2. Well I cannot find the glue.
3. Mel called "I found it."
4. My grandfather made this toy on May 3 1951.

Skills Practice

Write each sentence. Use commas where you need them.

1. The model fairs started on June 5 1976.
2. Do you go every year Tina?
3. Yes I like to build models.
4. Jake said "I went to the fair last year."
5. Ruth does your brother build model boats?
6. His boat won a prize on March 9 1980.
7. Tina asked "May I see the model boat?"

Writing Sentences

Write four sentences using commas.

1. Write one sentence that names a friend and asks him or her about a favorite toy.
2. Write one sentence that tells your friend's answer. Use a conversation word and your friend's exact words.
3. Write a sentence that tells the month, day, and year that something was made.
4. Write a sentence that begins with the word *no*.

Sample Answer 1. The model fairs started on June 5, 1976.

Understanding New Words

Sometimes you may not know the meaning of a word in a sentence. You can look up the word in the dictionary. You can also look at the other words in the sentence. Sometimes the other words help you understand the meaning of a word.

● Read this sentence.

They gave me a nice *reward* for finding the puppy.

Suppose you did not know the meaning of *reward*. Read the sentence again. The other words in the sentence give you an idea of what *reward* means. A *reward* is something given to you in return for something good that you did.

Sometimes you have to read the sentences before and after the word to find its meaning. The other sentences can help make the meaning of the word clear.

● Read these sentences.

Nicky thinks the soup tastes good.
Dolores thinks so, too.
She *agrees* with Nicky.

Read the sentences again. They tell you that both Nicky and Dolores like the soup. The word *agrees* tells you Dolores feels the same way about the soup as Nicky does.

Talk About It

Read each sentence. Try to find out the meaning of the underlined word.

1. My <u>assistant</u> will help me do the magic show.
2. I want to have a party to <u>celebrate</u> my birthday.
3. The fish is very <u>slippery</u>.
   The fish slid right out of my hand.
4. Tim just moved in.
   He is a <u>newcomer</u> on our street.

Skills Practice

Read each sentence. Write the underlined word in each sentence. Write what you think the word means.

1. Bill washed the shirt to <u>remove</u> the spot on it.
2. The balloon <u>burst</u> when I put too much air in it.
3. The fire <u>occurred</u> early in the morning.
4. I want a glass of water to drink. I am <u>thirsty</u>.
5. Myra did not sleep well.
   The bed had a lumpy <u>mattress</u>.
6. I put the letter in an <u>envelope</u>.
   Then I wrote your name and address on it.
7. Nana is my <u>companion</u>.
   She goes everywhere with me.

History of the English Language

Long ago there were only a few languages. One of these was called *Indo-European*. At first the people who spoke Indo-European all lived in one place. Then groups of people moved to new homes. They found different plants, animals, and weather. Slowly they made up new words and sounds to talk about these new things. After a while new languages took the place of Indo-European. Some languages that grew from Indo-European are English, Spanish, German, and French. We say that these languages belong to the Indo-European family.

● Look at the words from the Indo-European family of languages. How are they alike?

French	Spanish	German	Russian	English
mère	madre	mutter	mats	mother

People began speaking English in about the year 500 A.D. These people lived in England. Early English looked and sounded different from English today. We call early English *Old English*.

● Look at these Old English words. The *wh* in *what* and the *ir* in *bird* are turned around in the Old English words.

*hw*aet (*wh*at)   *br*id (*bir*d)   īs (ice)

A.D. **500**	**1066**	**1500**	**1961**
Old English warrior saying *Wes hāl*	French noble saying *Gretyings*	Explorer saying *Good day*	Astronaut saying *Hello*

In 1066 the French people fought a war with the English. The French won the war and brought new words to England. Old English changed to *Middle English*. Middle English looked more like the English you know, but it sounded different.

• Look at these Middle English words. Can you guess what they are?

yelow   redy   looke

After 1500 English began to look and sound more like English today. This English is called *Modern English*. English is still changing. New words help it change. Some modern English words are *astronaut, radar,* and *sonar.*

Talk About It

1. What English words fit into this chart?

	Spanish	German	French	English
	flor	Blume	fleur	
	sol	Sonne	soleil	
	estrella	Stern	astre	

2. Middle English often used the letter *y* where Modern English uses *i*. Spell these Middle English words in Modern English.

   a. wyse   b. myne   c. sayd   d. tyme

3. Imagine you live on another planet. Make up new words for the plants and animals there.

Skills Review

Read each sentence. Add more words to the subject part of each sentence. Then write your new sentence.

1. The circus arrives.
2. Traffic stops.
3. Neighbors watch.
4. Clowns pass.
5. Horses trot.
6. A monkey follows.
7. The crowd claps.
8. A baby laughs.

Read each sentence. Add more words to the predicate part of each sentence. Then write the new sentence.

9. Ms. Bridge measures.
10. My uncle cuts.
11. Paul sweeps.
12. Monica glues.
13. Two boys hammer.
14. Tina saws.
15. Her sister repairs.
16. Everyone builds.

Write each sentence. Use commas where you need them.

17. When did you learn to sail Rob?
18. Rob said "I started three years ago."

19. Well you must enjoy your new boat.
20. Yes my family built it.
21. We finished it on April 8 1981.
22. We took our first sail on June 9 1981.
23. Would you like to go for a sail Sue?
24. Yes that would be a lot of fun.

Read each sentence. Write the underlined word in each sentence. Write what you think the word means.

25. The kitten <u>trembled</u> as the noise grew louder.
26. We need to <u>breathe</u> air to live.
27. There were not many children at school.
    Only a <u>handful</u> came.
28. They went to the school play. We also <u>attended</u>.
29. Noise <u>disturbs</u> Max. Loud music bothers him too.

People first began to write books long ago. At that time, there were no exact rules for commas and periods. Readers often had to guess where the commas and periods belonged.

Here is a sentence with no commas. How many different people may be named?

Billy Joe Mary Jane Ann Marie and Lou went downtown.

Exploring Language

Fact and Opinion

You often read and hear what people have to say. Sometimes they state facts. A *fact* gives information that is true. Facts can also be checked. Sometimes people give opinions. An *opinion* tells what people think or feel.

The woman on TV is stating facts. You can check if the information about the rocket is true. All the children are giving opinions. They tell what they think or feel about the rocket trip.

Wayne and his sister went to the museum. Here are some things they said.

Birds lay eggs in their nests.
Some birds make nests from grass.
These are interesting birds.
Their feathers are beautiful.

● Read the sentences again. Which sentences state facts? Which give opinions?

Talk About It

Read each sentence. Does it state a fact or an opinion?

1. Many fish live in the sea.
2. Bluefish are the prettiest fish.
3. Scientists explore the sea.
4. Exploring the sea must be exciting.

Skills Practice

Write **fact** if the sentence states a fact. Write **opinion** if the sentence gives an opinion.

1. There are four seasons in the year.
2. Spring is the best season.
3. Flowers come out in the spring.
4. Leaves fall in the autumn.
5. Fall leaves are beautiful.
6. It is hot in the summer.
7. Maybe it will be cooler this summer.
8. Flowers need rain to grow.
9. The trees get wet when it rains.
10. Rain is awful.

Sample Answer 1. Fact

Ads

You have probably seen many ads before. *Ads* tell you about things you can buy. You can find ads on TV and radio. Newspapers and magazines also have ads. Some books have ads on their covers.

You'll love Circus Wheels. We've added nuts and fruits. Circus Wheels have important vitamins your body needs. They are good for you!

Many ads give facts. Facts give information that can be checked. Facts also give information that is helpful. Ads also state opinions. Opinions tell what someone thinks or feels.

- Look at the ad above. What does the ad tell you about? Which sentences state facts? Which sentences state opinions?

Here are sentences from another ad. This ad is on the cover of a book.

This book is about caring for your dog. It is the best book to read. The book tells how to train your dog. You'll enjoy reading this book.

- Look at the ad on the book cover again. What does the ad tell you about? Which sentences state facts? Which sentences state opinions?

Talk About It

Read this ad. Does each sentence state a fact or an opinion?

1. *Granny's Pies* are delicious!
2. They have vitamins.
3. They're better than any pies you've ever tasted.

Read this ad from a book jacket. Does each sentence state a fact or an opinion?

1. *Make Way for Ducklings* is a great book.
2. The family of ducks lives in Boston.
3. You'll love this story!
4. This story won an award.

Skills Practice

Read each ad. Write **fact** if the ad states a fact. Write **opinion** if it gives an opinion.

1. *Country Bread* is baked fresh everyday!
2. We make our bread with milk and flour.
3. We add butter, too.
4. Our bread is the best you can buy.
5. *Madeline* is the story of a little girl.
6. She lives in Paris.
7. This story is good.
8. The pictures are interesting.

Book Reports

Sometimes the ad on the jacket of a book makes you want to read the book. When you like a book you want your friends to read it, too.

A *book report* tells other people about a book you have read. The report is done a certain way. First you tell the name of the book. This is the book's *title*. Next you tell who wrote the book. This person is the *author*. Then you tell what the book is about.

There are many ways to tell about a book. You can describe the people that are in the book. You can tell the order of things that happen in the book.

● Look at this book report.

Name _Tom Harris_

My Book Report

Title _The House on Haunted Hill_

Author _Brian Murray_

In this book a family lives in a haunted house. The family does not know the house is haunted. One day a dish suddenly flies through the air. Next a strange

Notice that the title of the book was written at the top of the page. The author's name was written next. Then the paragraph told about the book.

The first sentence in the paragraph gave the main idea of the whole book. The other sentences told the order of things that happened in the book.

Notice that the book report did not tell the entire story. If it did, the report would be too long. Also, people might not read the book if they already knew everything that happened.

Talking About Book Reports

Read the book report on the other page.

1. What is the title of the book?
2. Who is the author?
3. What is the book about?
4. Did the paragraph describe a person or tell about things in time order?

Writing a Book Report

The information below belongs in a book report. But it is not in the right order. Write the information in the right order.

This book is about how to care for a dog.
I learned three things.
Last you must give your dog a nice place to sleep.
First you must feed a dog good food every day.
Next you must give your dog some exercise.
Lila Berger
Your New Dog

Practicing a Book Report

Thinking About A Book Report

Now you will write a book report. Choose a book you have read and liked. What will you tell about your book in the book report?

Writing a Book Report

Use this form to help you write your report.

Name _____

My Book Report

Title _____

Author _____

1. Write your name, the title of the book, and the name of the author on your paper.
2. Write a main idea sentence about the book. Remember to indent the first word.
3. Write a few detail sentences that tell what your book is about.

Edit Your Book Report

Read the book report. Think about these questions.

1. Did your book report tell something interesting about the book?
2. Did you use a good main idea sentence?
3. Did you spell the title of the book correctly? Did you spell the author's name correctly?
4. Did you use capital letters and periods correctly?

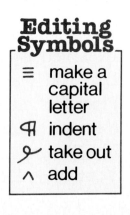

Editing Symbols

≡ make a capital letter

¶ indent

❨ take out

∧ add

A Book Talk

A book talk is another way to share a book. You can read your book report aloud or tell about the book in your own words. Follow these rules.

1. Look at the people in the class as you speak.
2. Speak loudly and clearly but not too fast.
3. Tell people where they can find the book.

Remember to be a good listener. Follow these rules.

1. Look at the person. Do not talk to other people.
2. Try to remember what the person is saying.
3. Ask questions about things you did not understand.

INDEPENDENT WRITING
A Book Report

Prewriting Suppose you were going to write an advertisement for your favorite book. You want people to read and enjoy the book. Read page 282 to help you plan your ad. What facts will you tell about your book? What opinions will you use? Make some notes. Use interesting words to attract the attention of the reader.

Writing Write an advertisement for your favorite book. Try to start your ad with an exciting sentence. Remember to tell the name of the book and the author. Then write detail sentences that tell what happened.

Editing Use the check questions and editing symbols on page 286 to edit your ad.

Unit Review

Write each sentence correctly. Then write **telling** if it is a telling sentence. Write **question** if it is a question sentence. Write **exclamation** if it is an exclamation sentence. *pages 262–263*

1. did you read this story
2. how hard I cried
3. i drew a picture
4. Do you like it
5. My picture is on the wall
6. What a good story it was

Read each sentence. Write the main word in the subject part. Then write **noun** if the word is a noun. Write **pronoun** if the word is a pronoun. *pages 264–265*

7. A girl went to see her grandmother.
8. She wore a red cape.
9. A wolf saw her in the forest.
10. He wanted her basket.
11. It was filled with food.

Read each sentence. Write the verb. *pages 266–267*

12. I play the piano.
13. My sister sings.
14. We enjoy music.
15. We practice every day.

Add words to the subject part of sentences 16, 17, and 18. Add words to the predicate part of sentences 19, 20, and 21. Then write each sentence. *pages 270–271*

16. The band played.
17. The children sang.
18. A girl danced.
19. People stood.
20. A man cheered.
21. A woman clapped.

Write each sentence. Use commas where you need them.

22. George are you going to the play?
23. Yes I am going next week.
24. Sam said "It was really good."
25. We have tickets for January 8 1983.

Write the underlined word in each sentence. Write
what you think the word means. *pages 274–275*

26. I forgot your book.
Please <u>remind</u> me to get it.

27. There is no one home.
I feel very <u>lonely</u>.

The information below belongs in a book report.
But it is not in the right order. Find the book's title
and author. Put the sentences in the right order. *pages 284–286*

28. a. The Monroe family took an interesting trip.
   b. The family started their trip in the fall.
   c. by Margaret Hope
   d. They got stuck in snow in the winter.
   e. Finally the Monroes returned home in the summer.
   f. A Year to Remember
   g. They traveled around the world in one year.
   h. Next the family got lost in the spring.

29. Write the book report.

Has anyone ever whispered in your ear? Sometimes you do not hear the whole message. In this story, whispering leads to one mix-up after another. All the animals know only one thing for sure. "It's a surprise!"

The Surprise Party

"I'm having a party tomorrow," whispered Rabbit.
"It's a surprise."

"Rabbit is hoeing the parsley tomorrow," whispered Owl.
"It's a surprise."

"Rabbit is going to sea tomorrow," whispered Squirrel.
"It's a surprise."

"Rabbit is climbing a tree tomorrow," whispered Duck.
"It's a surprise."

"Rabbit is riding a flea tomorrow," whispered Mouse. "It's a surprise."

"Rabbit is raiding the poultry tomorrow," whispered Fox. "It's a surprise."

"Reading poetry?" said Frog to himself.
"His own, I suppose. How dull."

The next day Rabbit went to see Frog.
"Come with me, Frog," he said.
"I have a surprise for you."
"No, thank you," said Frog.
"I know your poetry. It puts me to sleep."
And he hopped away.

So Rabbit went to see Fox.
"Come with me, Fox," he said.
"I have a surprise for you."
"No, thank you," said Fox.
"I don't want you raiding the poultry.
I'll get the blame."
And he ran off.

So Rabbit went to see Mouse.
"Come with me Mouse," he said.
"I have a surprise for you."
"No, thank you," said Mouse.
"A rabbit riding a flea?
Even I am too big for that."
And Mouse scampered away.

So Rabbit went to see Duck.
"Come with me, Duck," he
said.
"I have a surprise for you."
"No, thank you," said Duck.
"Mouse told me you were
climbing a tree.
Really, you're too old for
that sort of thing."
And Duck waddled off.

So Rabbit went to see Squirrel.
"Come with me, Squirrel,"
he said.
"I have a surprise for you."
"No, thank you," said Squirrel.
"I know you're going to sea,
but good-byes make me sad."
And Squirrel ran up the tree.

So Rabbit went to see Owl.
"Owl," he said, "I don't know what YOU think
I'm doing, but "I'M HAVING A PARTY."
And this time everyone heard clearly.
"A party!" they shouted. "Why didn't you say so?"
"A party! How nice!" And it was a nice party.
And such a surprise.

Pat Hutchins

Creative Activities

1. This story would make a good puppet play.
   Choose classmates to play the part of each
   animal. Each classmate will draw the animal he
   or she will play. Color the animals and cut them
   out. Your class will need some sticks or long,
   narrow pieces of wood. Fasten the animals to the
   stick. Act out the play using the puppets. Each
   classmate should read what the animal says in the
   story.

2. **Creative Writing**   Read the story again. Tell what
   words each animal changes in each message. Then
   write some other mixed-up messages. Here is one.

   "I am making a flower," whispered Bob.
   "Bob is taking a shower," whispered Dave.

Read each group of words in each pair. Write each group of words that is a sentence. *pages 2–3*

1. The dog barked.
   Barked the dog.
2. Ate hay an elephant.
   An elephant ate hay.

3. We fed the cat.
   Fed the cat we.
4. The duck away swam.
   The duck swam away.

Write each sentence correctly. Then write **telling** if it is a telling sentence. Write **question** if it is a question sentence. Write **exclamation** if it is an exclamation sentence. *pages 4–5, 6–7*

5. joe called Pete today.
6. can you go to Lee Park

7. what fun we can have
8. al will be here at noon

Look at the sentence part in the box. Write **subject** or **predicate** if it is a subject part or predicate part. *pages 10–11*

9. The children | watched the animals.
10. The sheep | nibbled grass.
11. The horse | walked toward the children.
12. The cows | followed the farmer.

Write each noun. Write **proper** if it is a proper noun. Write **common** if it is a common noun. *pages 48–49*

13. Ira went to Central Store.
14. Juan sang songs.
15. A dog followed Ira.
16. Inez walked to Hill Drive.

Write the name and address and each date correctly. *pages 50–53*

17. mrs h ortez
319 sterling road
houston texas 77007

18. may 16 1983
19. july 10 1981
20. april 24 1980

Write the verb in the past. *pages 84–85*

21. try　　**22.** wash　　**23.** call　　**24.** fix

Write the second sentence using the correct pronoun. *pages 116–117*

25. The boys clean the floor.
＿＿ need a can of wax.
26. Pearl dusts the room.
＿＿ uses a cloth.

27. Dad washes the car.
＿＿ finds the pail.
28. Mom and I rake leaves.
＿＿ have fun.

Write the correct verb in each sentence. *pages 118–119*

29. They ＿＿ the stairs.　(sweep, sweeps)
30. He ＿＿ the bed.　(make, makes)
31. I ＿＿ the dishes.　(wash, washes)
32. She ＿＿ the glasses.　(dry, dries)

Read each sentence. Write the second sentence
using the correct possessive pronoun. *pages 120–121*

33. George fixed the car.
＿＿ brother helped.　(His, Its)
34. Tom and I went to the game.
＿＿ parents went also.　(Their, Our)
35. Sue and Carol baked last night.
＿＿ bread was delicious.　(Her, Their)

Write each sentence correctly. Put quotation marks and commas where they belong. *pages 122–123*

36. George called are you ready?
37. Jane replied we can go now
38. Sam said bring a jacket
39. Jan added don't forget your gloves

Look at the noun in ( ). Use the possessive form of the noun in the blank. Write the possessive noun. *pages 154–155, 158–159*

40. The ___ bikes had bells.   (boys)
41. One ___ bike had a flag.   (girl)
42. The ___ bike had a horn.   (woman)

Write each sentence correctly. Use a capital letter to begin each important word in a proper noun. *pages 162–163*

43. I swim in june and july.   **45.** This sunday is mother's day.
44. We had fun on friday.   **46.** I saw you in april.

Write each adjective and the noun it describes. *pages 184–185*

47. I saw a red balloon.   **49.** The dog had sad eyes.
48. A little boy held it.   **50.** A big girl threw a ball.

Write the correct adjective to fill each blank. *pages 188–189*

51. Bev found an old coin.
     Bob found an ___ coin than Bev's.   (older, oldest)
52. Miguel got the ___ coin of all.   (older, oldest)
53. Sue had a soft pillow.
     Lois had a ___ pillow.   (softest, softer)

Write each verb. Then write whether the verb is in
the **present,** the **past,** or the **future.** *pages 222–223*

54. Rita played golf.
55. She will play again soon.

56. Rita tries very hard.
57. She learns quickly.

Write the verb that names an action in the past. *pages 224–225*

58. I ___ the bus.   (see)
59. Lisa ___ lunch.   (eat)

60. Two girls ___ home.   (go)
61. I ___ , too.   (do)

Write the correct form of the verb. *pages 226–227*

62. Liz has ___ home.   (go)
63. She has ___ dinner.   (eat)

64. I have ___ Joe.   (see)
65. Val has ___ well.   (do)

Write each sentence. Draw a line under the adverb
in each sentence. Draw two lines under the verb
that the adverb describes. *pages 232–233, 234–235*

66. Yesterday we went on a picnic.
67. Suddenly it rained.

68. We packed up quickly.

69. Then we drove home.

Write each sentence correctly. Put commas where
they belong. *pages 272–273*

70. Mother asked "Are you leaving soon?"
71. Yes we must be ready in an hour.
72. Don't forget your books Jane.
73. Mother I will remember.

Handbook Contents

I. Grammar and Usage

Sentences

DEFINITION

A **sentence** is a group of words that states a
complete idea. page 2   MORE PRACTICE, page 307

The farmer grows food for people.

Many animals live on a farm.

KINDS OF SENTENCES

A **telling sentence** is a sentence that tells something. page 4 MORE PRACTICE, pages 307, 313
A robin built a nest.   The bird sings to me.

A **question sentence** is a sentence that asks something. page 4 MORE PRACTICE, pages 307, 313
Why do birds sing?   Did you plant the tree?

An **exclamation sentence** is a sentence that shows strong feeling. page 4 MORE PRACTICE, pages 307, 313
How pretty the song is!   What a tall tree that is!

PART OF SENTENCES

The **subject part** of a sentence names whom or what the sentence is about. page 10 MORE PRACTICE, pages 308, 313, 321
Rosa jumped rope.   The children played tag.

The **predicate part** of a sentence tells what action the subject part does. page 10 MORE PRACTICE, pages 308, 313
The cat pawed the sofa.   Jack chased the cat.

Parts of Speech

NOUN

A **noun** is a word that names a person, a place, or a thing. page 36 MORE PRACTICE, pages 308-309, 313, 321
The neighbor came to our house.
The door blew shut in my face.

A **singular noun** is a noun that names one person, place, or thing. page 40 MORE PRACTICE, pages 309, 315
A child threw a ball.
An old woman walked by the house.

A **plural noun** is a noun that names more than one person, place, or thing. Most plural nouns end with **s** or **es.** pages 40, 42 MORE PRACTICE, pages 309, 315
The wild animals sat in the cages.
Tami put the kittens in two boxes.

Use **the** before singular or plural nouns.   page 191   MORE PRACTICE, page 317

Joanna set the table.

Mother washed the dishes.

Use **a** and **an** before singular nouns only. Use **an** before words that begin with vowel sounds. Use **a** before words that begin with all other sounds.   page 191   MORE PRACTICE, page 317

Alice saw a squirrel in a tree.

She saw it eating an acorn.

A **common noun** is a noun that names any person, place or thing.   page 48   MORE PRACTICE, page 310

The boy plays with a dog.

The dog sleeps under the bench.

A **proper noun** is a noun that names a special person, place or thing. Each important word in a proper noun begins with a capital letter.   page 48   MORE PRACTICE, pages 310, 315

Many people visited the Old West Museum.

Karen Cook works in a store.

A **possessive noun** is a noun that names whom or what has something.   page 150   MORE PRACTICE, page 316

Grandfather fixed Tom's bike.

He moved the children's toys.

PRONOUN

A **pronoun** is a word that takes the place of one or more nouns.   page 116   MORE PRACTICE, pages 314, 321

She threw the ball.

We went to the game.

They like football.

Did you see the game?

He caught the pass.

I enjoy playing tennis.

It is fun.

A **possessive pronoun** is a pronoun that shows who or what has or owns something. page 120 MORE PRACTICE, page 314

My sister is an artist.   Her studio is in the city.

Your dad is a writer.   His book is interesting.

Its photographs are beautiful.   Our friends read it.

Their parents read the book also.

VERB

A **verb** is a word that names an action. page 70 MORE PRACTICE, pages 311, 313, 321

The children jump.   Michael moves his chair.

A **verb in the present** names an action that happens now. page 74 MORE PRACTICE, pages 311, 319

Now the boy throws a ball.   The dog swims after the ball.

Add **-s** to most verbs in the present when they work with singular nouns. page 78 MORE PRACTICE, pages 311, 312, 319

Mother rides a bus to work.   Father walks to his office.

Do not change verbs in the present to make them work with plural nouns. page 79 MORE PRACTICE, pages 311-312

The cowboys saddle the horses.   The animals kick the doors.

A **verb in the past** names an action that happened before. page 82 MORE PRACTICE, pages 312, 319

Yesterday, the bus stopped.

The children climbed the steps.

Add **-ed** to most verbs to make a verb in the past. page 84 MORE PRACTICE, pages 312, 319

The band marched.   People called to the band.

The **future tense of a verb** names an action that will take place in the future. page 222 MORE PRACTICE, page 319

Joan will swim in the race today.

Pedro will read three books this week.

A **helping verb** is a word that helps a verb to name an action. page 222 MORE PRACTICE, page 320

The family has moved to another city.

They have lived here for years.

Add **-ed** to most verbs when you use them with the
helping verb **have** or **has.**   page 226   MORE PRACTICE, page 320
You have learned the rules.
Robert has played the game many times.

ADJECTIVE

An **adjective** is a word that describes a noun.   page 184   MORE
Little Tommy lives in a big house.   PRACTICE, page 317
Beautiful flowers grow along the green fence.

Add **-er** to an adjective to compare one thing with
another.   page 188   MORE PRACTICE, page 317
John saw a taller tree than Sue did.

Add **-est** to an adjective to compare several things.   page 188
Jane found the tallest tree of all.   MORE PRACTICE, page 317

ADVERB

An **adverb** is a word that describes
an action.   pages 232, 234   MORE PRACTICE, page 320
Greg loaded the cart carefully.   Then he delivered the packages.

II. Mechanics

Capitalization

Use a **capital letter** to begin the first word of
every sentence.   page 6   MORE PRACTICE, pages 308, 313
The bride carried white flowers.   People waved at the car.

Begin each important word in a proper noun with
a capital letter.   page 48   MORE PRACTICE, pages 310, 315, 316
Mr. Frank Hess builds houses for people.
The Doyles stopped to eat at Joe's Diner.

Begin a **title** with a capital letter. End most titles with a
period.   page 50   MORE PRACTICE, page 310
Dr. William Barnes cares for sick persons.
Ms. Martha Herr teaches the third grade.

An **initial** is the first letter of a name. Write an initial with a capital letter. Put a period after the letter. page 50

Maria L. Garcia is my friend.
T. H. White writes books.

Use **capital letters** to begin proper nouns that name places. page 52 MORE PRACTICE, pages 310, 315

The family visited San Diego, California.
The Mississippi River flows south.

Punctuation

Use a **period (.)** at the end of a telling sentence. page 6
MORE PRACTICE, pages 308, 313
A heavy rain fell in the morning.
The Anderson family played games.

Use a **question mark (?)** at the end of a question sentence. page 7 MORE PRACTICE, pages 308, 313
Will you buy a bird?   Who bought the bird?

Use an **exclamation mark (!)** at the end of an exclamation sentence. page 7 MORE PRACTICE, pages 308, 313
How small the bird is!   What a big building!

Put a **comma (,)** between the name of the city and the state when you write them together. page 52
MORE PRACTICE, page 310
I live in Waco, Texas.
You live in Athens, Ohio

Use a **comma (,)** to separate the day of the month from the year. page 53 MORE PRACTICE, pages 310, 322
January 3, 1982   April 10, 1981

Use a **comma (,)** to set off words such as *yes, no,* and *well* when they begin in a sentence. page 272 MORE PRACTICE,
page 322
No, I can't go tonight. Well, perhaps next time.

Use a **comma (,)** to set off the name of a person who is spoken to directly in a sentence. page 272
MORE PRACTICE, page 322
George, I'll be right there.
Are you coming, Carl?

Add an **apostrophe** and **-s ('s)** to write the possessive of most singular nouns. page 152 MORE PRACTICE, page 316

What is the boy's name?
Jack took the giant's gold.

Add an **apostrophe (')** to write the possessive of most plural nouns. page 153 MORE PRACTICE, page 316

Aunt Jenny sewed the girls' dresses.
Then she ironed the boys' pants.

Use an **apostrophe (')** in a contraction to take the place of the letter or letters that are left out. page 236

MORE PRACTICE, page 321

Don't write in this book.
I can't find my pencil.

Capitalization and Punctuation in Conversations

Put **quotation marks (" ")** around the words that each person says. page 122 MORE PRACTICE, page 315

   Stacy said, "I want to read another story."

Use a **conversation word** such as *said, whispered,* or *called* to tell how the person talked. Use a **comma (,)** after the conversation word. page 122 MORE PRACTICE, page 315

   Jay answered, "Choose another book from the shelf."

Put a **period** before the last quotation mark at the end of the sentence. page 122 MORE PRACTICE, page 315

   Mike added, "There's a funny story in that book."

Indent the first word each time a new person talks. page 122

MORE PRACTICE, page 315

→Susan called, "I like this story more."

Capitalize the first word in each quotation. page 122 MORE PRACTICE,

page 315

   Jay stated, "We will read them all."

III. Spelling

Spelling Nouns

To make most singular nouns plural, add **-s.** page 42 MORE PRACTICE, page 309

boy	girl	wagon
boys	girls	wagons

If a singular noun ends with **s, ss, x, ch,** or **sh,** add **-es** to write the plural. page 42 MORE PRACTICE, page 309

lunch	bus	fox
lunches	buses	foxes

If a singular noun ends with a consonant and **y**, change the **y** to **i** and add **-es** to write the plural. page 43 MORE PRACTICE, page 309

baby	penny	city
babies	pennies	cities

Spelling Verbs

If a verb ends in **s, ss, ch, sh,** or **x,** add **-es** to make the verb in the present work with a singular noun. page 78 MORE PRACTICE, pages 312, 319

toss	catch	fix
tosses	catches	fixes

If a verb ends with a consonant and **y,** change the **y** and **i** and add -**es** to make the correct form of the present. page 79 MORE PRACTICE, pages 312, 319

cry	try	hurry
cries	tries	hurries

If the verb ends with a consonant and **y,** change the **y** to **i** and add -**ed** to make a verb in the past. page 84 MORE PRACTICE, pages 312, 319

cry	hurry	try
cried	hurried	tried

If a verb ends with **e,** drop the **-e** and add **-ed** to make the correct form of the past. page 84 MORE PRACTICE, pages 312, 319

shape	use	vote
shaped	used	voted

Spelling Adjectives

If a word ends with consonant, vowel, consonant, double the last consonant and add **-y** to form the adjective. page 196 MORE PRACTICE, page 318

fun	mud	sun
funny	muddy	sunny

IV. Vocabulary

A **compound word** is a word made up of two other words. page 161

sunshine→sun + shine   baseball→base + ball

A **synonym** is a word that has nearly the same meaning as another word. page 194 MORE PRACTICE, page 318

Trees grow in the forest.
Trees grow in the woods.
The race began at noon.
The race started at noon.

An **antonym** is a word that means the opposite of another word. page 195 MORE PRACTICE, page 318

The little bears slept.
The big bears slept.
Bob wears his old shirt.
Bob wears his new shirt.

A **contraction** is a word made up of two words.
The words are joined together to make one word.
One or more letters are left out. page 236 MORE PRACTICE, page 321

You're very kind to me.
Lily isn't out of bed yet.

A **prefix** is a group of letters added to the beginning of a word. page 238

The unhappy child cried.
You must rewrite the lesson.

Learning About Sentences, pages 2–3
Read the groups of words in each pair. Write each
group of words that is a sentence.

1. Many animals live here.
Many animals.

2. A squirrel.
A squirrel eats a nut.

3. A rabbit eats the grass.
A rabbit.

4. The birds build a nest.
The birds.

5. Some ducks.
Some ducks walk away.

6. A fish.
A fish swims in the pond.

7. A frog jumps on a rock.
A frog.

8. A cat sees a mouse.
A cat.

9. Two dogs.
Two dogs bark at a cat.

10. Some people walk quickly.
Some people.

Three Kinds of Sentences, pages 4–5
Read each sentence. Write **telling** if it is a telling
sentence. Write **question** if it is a question sentence.
Write **exclamation** if it is an exclamation sentence.

1. We went to the pet store.
2. How small that puppy is!
3. Did you hear the bird?
4. What a pretty song it sings!
5. I liked the little monkey.
6. The monkey sat on my arm.
7. Did you see the kittens?
8. Did you buy a pet?
9. I bought a kitten.
10. What does it look like?
11. It is gray and white.
12. What did you name it?
13. We call it Fluffy.
14. How cute Fluffy is!
15. Fluffy likes to play.
16. How soft the fur is!

Capitalizing and Punctuating Sentences, pages 6–7

Some special signs are missing in each sentence.
Write each sentence correctly.

1. many bats live in caves
2. how dark this cave is!
3. When do bats hunt
4. they hunt at night.
5. What do bats eat

6. Bats hang upside down
7. bears live in caves.
8. Many sleep all winter
9. what a big bear that is
10. can you run fast

Parts of Telling Sentences, pages 10–11

Read each sentence. Look at the part in the box.
Write **subject** if it is a subject part. Write **predicate**
if it is a predicate part.

1. The frog | found a ball.
2. A princess | lost it.
3. The frog | tossed the ball.
4. The princess | ran home.

5. The frog | knocked loudly.
6. The frog | came in.
7. The frog | sat quietly.
8. The frog | became a prince.

Learning About Nouns, pages 36-39

Write each sentence. Draw a line under each noun.

1. Jan went to the station.
2. Mother carried her bag.
3. Father bought a ticket.
4. Jan climbed on the bus.
5. A driver took the ticket.
6. Jan found a seat.

7. Jan sat near a window.
8. Her little brother waved.
9. The bus left the station.
10. A truck passed the bus.
11. Aunt Sue met Jan in town.
12. Uncle Bob waved to Jan.

Singular and Plural Nouns, pages 40–41

Write each sentence with the correct noun.

1. Two ___ got on the bus.   (boy, boys)
2. They rode to a little ___.   (town, towns)
3. They stopped at three ___.   (store, stores)
4. Jim bought a ___ for his bike.   (bell, bells)
5. Fred bought a ___.   (game, games)
6. They also bought two ___.   (apple, apples)
7. A ___ passed them.   (truck, trucks)

Forming Plural Nouns, pages 42–44

Write the plural of each noun.

1. train
2. bus
3. woman
4. watch
5. baby
6. box
7. class
8. dish
9. tooth
10. goose
11. car
12. airplane
13. child
14. family
15. foot

Making New Words, page 45

Change the underlined word in each pair of sentences to tell what kind of work the person does. Write the second sentence with the new word.

1. Lee <u>paints</u> houses.
   Lee is a ___.
2. Tom <u>sings</u> old songs.
   Tom is a ___.
3. Ginny <u>dances</u> in the show.
   Ginny is a ___.
4. Mary <u>writes</u> books.
   Mary is a ___.

Proper and Common Nouns, pages 48–49

Write each sentence. Underline each noun. Write
proper if it is a proper noun. Write **common** if it is
a common noun.

1. Amy Gold rides her bike in Central Park.
2. A boy plays ball in the schoolyard.
3. Kevin walks his dog on Main Street.
4. Miss Yan bought a new car in June.
5. Jan drove the car to Arizona.

Writing Names, Addresses, and Dates, pages 50–54

Write each name and address correctly.

1.
jose rivera
29 hillside avenue
houston, texas 77039

2.
dr anna feng
16 willow road
denver colorado 80220

3.
mr paul rosen
34 hudson street
portland, maine 04101

4.
ms micco crow
46 maple drive
mobile alabama 36608

Write each date correctly.

5. june 3 1957
6. august 10 1962
7. march 12 1979
8. february 23 1978

9. october 8 1975
10. january 5 1981
11. april 2 1983
12. november 17 1982

Learning About Verbs, pages 70–71

Read each sentence. If the underlined word is a verb, write **verb.** If the underlined word is not a verb, write **not verb.**

1. Lee <u>reads</u> a book.
2. Randy turns the <u>pages.</u>
3. A boy <u>laughs</u> at a story.
4. Jake <u>jumps</u> rope.
5. Lisa turns the <u>rope.</u>
6. A dog <u>runs</u> by.

Verbs in Sentences, pages 72–73

Write each sentence. Underline the verb.

1. The girls play football.
2. Tom talks to the coach.
3. A man blows a whistle.
4. Carla kicks the ball.
5. The crowd cheers.
6. People jump up.

Verbs in the Present, pages 74–75

Read each sentence. Write **present** if the verb is in the present. Write **not present** if the verb is not.

1. Beth rides to the park.
2. A woman carries a baby.
3. Children played games.
4. A man sells balloons.
5. Two boys watch.
6. Jeff dropped the ball.

Using Verbs in the Present, pages 76–77

Write each sentence. Use the correct verb.

1. Sally ____ in the pool.   (swim, swims)
2. The boys ____ in the water.   (jump, jumps)
3. A girl ____ into the pool.   (dive, dives)
4. The girls ____ tag in the water.   (play, plays)

Spelling Verbs, pages 78–79

Write each sentence. Use the verb in the present.

1. Kim ___ a butterfly.   (chase)
2. Her sister ___ a net.   (carry)
3. Two boys ___ them.   (follow)
4. Roger ___ a frog.   (catch)
5. Two frogs ___ into the water.   (jump)
6. Roger ___ at them.   (laugh)

Verbs in the Past, pages 82–83

Read each sentence. Write **past** if the verb is in the past. Write **not past** if the verb is not.

7. Don jumped over the fence.
8. Sam plays hockey.
9. Jane hit the ball so far.
10. Jim chased after the ball.
11. Susan swims across the lake.
12. Carl pulled the wagon.

Spelling Verbs in the Past, pages 84–85

Write each sentence. Use the verb in the past.

1. Jimmy ___ to make a basket.   (learn)
2. Ronnie ___ the sofa.   (move)
3. The teacher ___ a funny movie.   (show)
4. A girl ___ to sing a song.   (try)
5. Inéz ___ the song.   (like)
6. Tom ___ me for his team.   (pick)

Reviewing Kinds of Sentences, pages 108–109

Some special signs are missing in each sentence.
Write each sentence correctly.

1. the keeper feeds a tiger
2. A lion roars
3. did you hear the lion?
4. how loud it is!

5. two men clean the cages
6. a woman sells balloons.
7. did you buy a balloon
8. what a big balloon it is

Complete Sentences, pages 110–111

Write each sentence. Draw a line between the
subject part and the predicate part.

1. The girls went fishing.
2. Ming rowed the boat.
3. Sandy caught a big fish.
4. A girl made a fire.

5. Henry cooked the fish.
6. The children saved money.
7. Elena walked the dog.
8. The dog barked at a bird.

Nouns and Verbs in Sentences, pages 112–113

Write each sentence. Draw one line under each
noun. Draw two lines under each verb.

1. A boy wrote a story.
2. A girl painted picture.
3. The class watched.
4. The teacher laughed.
5. Some children played.
6. The woman sang a song.
7. A man played the piano.
8. The dancers bowed.

9. The actors performed.
10. A child rode the bike.
11. The boys ran home.
12. The girls baked bread.
13. The men pushed the car.
14. The painter left early.
15. The people arrived.
16. Parents came to school.

Pronouns in Sentences, pages 116–117

Look at the underlined words. Use the correct pronoun to take their place. Write the new sentence.

1. <u>Debra</u> picked some peas.
   ____ cooked them.
2. <u>The peas</u> are sweet.
   ____ taste good.
3. <u>Tom</u> picked apples.
   ____ baked a pie.
4. <u>The pie</u> is done.
   ____ is hot.

Using Pronouns and Verbs, pages 118–119

Use the correct verb in each sentence. Write the sentence.

1. We ____ to school.   (walk, walks)
2. She ____ a car.   (drive, drives)
3. He ____ the bus.   (take, takes)
4. You ____ in a store.   (work, works)
5. I ____ on a farm.   (live, lives)
6. They ____ us pick corn.   (help, helps)
7. It ____ very tall.   (grow, grows)

Possessive Pronouns, pages 120–121

Write the second sentence using the correct pronoun.

1. Max paints houses.
   ____ painters work hard.
2. Max and I mix the paint.
   ____ hands get dirty.
3. Cindy wants a green door.
   ____ house is white.
4. The house is big.
   ____ doors are open.

Punctuating a Conversation, pages 122–123

Write each sentence. Add punctuation and capital
letters where they belong.

1. Dad stated I can't find your brother
2. Robin answered he is in the yard
3. Bob added Tommy is cutting the grass
4. Dad said go help him
5. Bob and Robin replied we will

Reviewing Nouns, pages 148–149

Write each sentence. Underline each noun. Write
singular if the noun is singular. Write **plural** if the
noun is plural.

1. A girl picked flowers.
2. The boy saw a butterly.
3. The butterfly had wings.
4. Two birds sang songs.
5. One bird flew fast.
6. A cat climbed a tree.
7. A turtle sat on a rock.
8. A cat saw the turtle.
9. Cats jumped on the rock.
10. Two dogs saw the cats.
11. A dog chased squirrels.
12. A squirrel ran up a tree.

Write each sentence correctly. Use a capital letter
to begin each important word in a proper noun.

1. pam planted a garden.
2. miss gomez helped.
3. sue went to lake school.
4. john pulled the weeds.
5. bob watered the lawn.
6. peter sold roses to ann.
7. mrs. fine bought some.
8. juan lives on oak road.
9. fisher hall is big.
10. joe cut the grass.

Possessive Nouns, pages 150–155

Decide if the noun in ( ) is singular or plural. Then use the possessive form of the noun in the blank. Write the sentence.

1. The ____ cat had kittens.   (girls)
2. The ____ kittens are funny.   (cat)
3. Kurt lost his ____ ball.   (friend)
4. He looked in the ____ box.   (cat)
5. The ____ ball belonged to Roy.   (kittens)
6. Kurt returned ____ ball.   (Roy)
7. The girls gave ____ toy to the kittens.   (John)
8. The kittens chased after the ____ laces.   (boys)

Possessive Nouns with Special Endings, pages 158–159

Look at the noun in ( ). Use the possessive form of the noun in the blank. Write the sentence.

1. The ____ cat cried all night.   (child)
2. I just saw the ____ new car.   (men)
3. The ____ tails are very long.   (mice)
4. The ____ club met last evening.   (women)
5. We could see the ____ nests.   (geese)
6. The ____ hat fell to the ground.   (man)
7. The ____ dress is very pretty.   (woman)

Capitalizing Days, Months, and Special Days, pages 162–163

Write each sentence. Use capital letters correctly.

1. This monday is halloween.
2. Does august begin today?
3. We played on saturday.
4. Today is new year's day.

Adjectives, pages 184–187

Read each sentence. Write the adjective. Then write the noun it describes.

1. There is a tall tree.
2. A gray squirrel climbs.
3. It has a bushy tail.
4. A big bird flies away.
5. It has a yellow beak.
6. I found a smooth stone.
7. I dropped a shiny coin.
8. We felt the cold water.
9. An orange fish swam by.
10. A little girl sat down.

Adjectives That Compare, pages 188–189

Choose the correct adjective to fill each blank. Then write the sentence.

1. Rosa saved old baseball cards.
   Jorge had an ___ card than Rosa's.   (older, oldest)
2. Mark found the ___ card of all.   (older, oldest)
3. We took a long walk.
   Pam took a ___ walk than ours.   (longer, longest)
4. Paul took the ___ walk of all.   (longer, longest)
5. Howard had a low voice.
   George had a ___ voice than Howard's.   (lower, lowest)
6. Carl had the ___ voice of all.   (lower, lowest)

Articles, page 191

Complete each sentence. Use a correct article.
Write the sentence.

1. I have ___ bicycle.
2. My aunt has ___ orange.
3. We ride down ___ street.
4. Sara eats ___ apple.
5. ___ apples grow on trees.
6. We have ___ big basket.

Synonyms, page 194

Use a synonym for the underlined word. Write the new sentence.

1. Beth is a <u>nice</u> person.
2. She makes <u>pretty</u> hats.
3. Jon is a very <u>smart</u> boy.
4. A <u>big</u> dog barked.
5. An <u>unhappy</u> baby cried.
6. The <u>noisy</u> child yelled.

Antonyms, page 195

Use an antonym for the underlined word. Write the new sentence.

1. I had an <u>open</u> umbrella.
2. She wore an <u>old</u> coat.
3. I took off my <u>wet</u> shoes.
4. I need a <u>soft</u> pillow.
5. I am a <u>slow</u> worker.
6. He sewed a <u>new</u> pillow.

Making Adjectives, pages 196–197

Make the word in ( ) into an adjective. Complete the sentence with the adjective. Write the sentence.

1. I have a ___ cat.   (fur)
2. I saw a ___ hill.   (rock)
3. It is a ___ night.   (fog)
4. She ate ___ soup.   (salt)
5. It was a ___ day.   (sun)
6. We wore ___ boots.   (dust)
7. He has ___ hands.   (dirt)
8. I have ___ fingers.   (stick)

Words That Sound the Same, pages 198–199

Choose the word with the correct meaning for each sentence. Write the sentence.

1. Do you ___ the bird?   (hear, here)
2. Do you ___ who is visiting our class?   (no, know)
3. Don't forget to ___ a note to your mother.   (write, right)
4. Are you going ___ , Jane?   (two, to, too)

Verbs in the Present and Past, pages 220–221

Use the correct verb in the present. Write the sentence.

1. Dan ___ home. (rush)
2. He ___ hard. (try)
3. A friend ___ by. (pass)

4. Joan ___ her bike. (fix)
5. She ___ Toby. (race)
6. Toby ___ fast. (ride)

Use the correct verb in the past. Write the sentence.

1. We ___ tennis. (play)
2. I ___ the ball. (toss)
3. You ___ to it. (race)

4. They ___ later. (watch)
5. A player ___. (kick)
6. You ___ then. (worry)

Verbs in the Future, pages 222–223

Write each verb. Then write whether each verb is in the **present,** the **past,** or the **future.**

1. Joan raced today.
2. She will race later.
3. Joan runs fast.

4. Todd will swim today.
5. He won a race earlier.
6. Todd swims well.

Using Verbs in the Past, pages 224–225

Write each sentence. Use the verb that names an action in the past.

1. The dogs ___ home. (go)
2. They ___ a meal. (eat)
3. A girl ___ them. (see)
4. The boys ___ not. (do)
5. They ___ away. (go)

6. I ___ a bone to one. (give)
7. My cat ___ fast. (grow)
8. I ___ your friend. (know)
9. The cat ___ a nap. (take)
10. The dog ___ to bark. (begin)

Helping Verbs, pages 226–227

Write the helping verb and the verb.

1. We have played ball.
2. You have enjoyed it.
3. Sue has improved a lot.
4. Ed has started a team.
5. They have walked away.
6. Brian has talked to me.
7. I have joined.
8. Kim has thanked me.
9. They have wanted players.
10. We have learned a lot.

More Verbs in the Past, pages 228–229

Write each sentence. Use the correct form of the verb.

1. Margie has ___ to the zoo.   (go)
2. She has ___ many wild animals.   (see)
3. Many birds have ___ past her.   (fly)
4. A little brown monkey has ___ a banana.   (take)
5. Margie has ___ to feel tired.   (begin)
6. She has ___ all her lunch.   (eat)

Adverbs, pages 232–235

Write each sentence. Draw a line under the adverb in each sentence. Then draw two lines under the verb each adverb describes.

1. We awakened early.
2. Jack dressed rapidly.
3. I dressed slowly.
4. Then we ate breakfast.
5. I brushed my teeth next.
6. Jack washed dishes fast.
7. Finally the bus arrived.
8. Mother called excitedly.
9. I grabbed my bag quickly.
10. We ran anxiously.

Contractions, pages 236–237

Write each sentence using a contraction for the underlined words.

1. I <u>can</u> <u>not</u> swim in deep water.
2. He <u>does</u> <u>not</u> like cold water.
3. Our friends <u>do</u> <u>not</u> want to race.
4. A little girl <u>did</u> <u>not</u> stay.
5. She <u>has</u> <u>not</u> learned to swim yet.
6. We <u>have</u> <u>not</u> been at the pool all day.

Nouns and Pronouns in the Subject Part, pages 264–265

Write the main word in the subject part. Write **noun** if the word is a noun. Write **pronoun** if the word is a pronoun.

1. The birds sing songs.
2. Father likes to sing.
3. He made up a song.
4. I sang with him.
5. Mother laughed.
6. She did a little dance.
7. A neighbor joined us.
8. We danced around.

Verbs in Sentences, pages 266–267

Write each sentence. Underline the verb.

1. I went to a party.
2. Gail made my costume.
3. She painted a paper bag.
4. She cut two holes in it.
5. I made funny noises.
6. My friends laughed.
7. We played games.
8. We enjoyed the party.

Building Sentences, pages 270-271

Add words to the subject part in sentences 1 to 4.
Add words to the predicate part in sentences 5 to 8.
Then write the sentence.

1. The window broke.
2. A man shouted.
3. The children ran.
4. A baby cried.

5. The snow fell.
6. The boys played.
7. Mother called.
8. The sun set.

Commas, pages 272–273

Write each sentence. Use commas where you need them.

1. Our friends arrived on January 10 1983.
2. Don called "They are getting out of the car."
3. Jody go open the front door for them.
4. Yes I will do it right now.
5. Help them with their bags Greg.
6. Well we are very happy to see you again.

Understanding New Words, pages 274-275

Read each sentence. Write the underlined word in each sententce. Write what you think the word means.

1. Becky had an <u>accident</u>. She fell down the stairs.
2. The shirt was a <u>bargain</u>. It was on sale.

3. Rico has a good <u>imagination</u>. He pretends he can fly.
4. The apartment is <u>vacant</u>. The family moved out.

Workbook

Learning About Sentences pages 2-3

A **sentence** is a group of words that states a complete idea.
A rabbit eats carrots.

Read the groups of words in each pair. Write the group of words that is a sentence.

1. A robin sings a song.
   A robin.
2. A skunk.
   A skunk has a stripe.
3. A squirrel.
   A squirrel buries nuts.
4. The raccoon wears a mask.
   The raccoon.

5. A deer.
   A deer drinks water.
6. The fox crosses the stream.
   The fox.
7. A groundhog sees a shadow.
   A groundhog.
8. The animals.
   The animals like the forest.

Three Kinds of Sentences pages 4-5

A **telling** sentence is a sentence that tells something.
Gorillas usually walk on four legs.

A **question** sentence is a sentence that asks something.
Can lions climb trees?

An **exclamation** sentence is a sentence that shows strong feeling.
What graceful animals leopards are!

Write each sentence. Write **telling** if it is a telling sentence. Write **question** if it is a question sentence. Write **exclamation** if it is an exclamation sentence.

1. Does the elephant eat peanuts?
2. Camels live in deserts.
3. When do owls sleep?
4. What good climbers monkeys are!

5. Does the leopard have spots?
6. What color are the stripes?
7. A zebra has stripes.
8. How fast the cheetah runs!

Workbook

Capitalizing and Punctuating Sentences pages 6-7

> Use a **capital letter** to begin the first word of every sentence.
>
> Use a **period (.)** at the end of a telling sentence.
> Elephants like people.
>
> Use a **question mark (?)** at the end of a question sentence.
> Where is the zebra cage?
>
> Use an **exclamation mark (!)** at the end of an exclamation sentence.
> What fun zoos are!

Write each sentence correctly. Some special signs are missing in each sentence.

1. how I love lions
2. can lions climb trees
3. most wild lions live in Africa
4. how large do lions grow
5. the lion makes its den in a hidden spot
6. lions usually sleep during the day
7. do they hunt at night
8. what powerful legs lions have
9. are lions distant cousins of the house cat
10. how cute lion cubs are
11. lions frighten many wild animals
12. how loudly lions roar
13. a mother lion feeds her cubs
14. are baby lions playful

Parts of Telling Sentences pages 10-11

> The **subject part** of a sentence names whom or what the sentence is about.
>
> The **predicate part** of a sentence tells what action the subject part does.
>   Penguins build nests on land.

Write each sentence. Draw a line under the subject part. Draw two lines under the predicate part.

1. Most penguins live near the South Pole.
2. Penguins swim long distances.
3. Penguins walk in a clumsy way.
4. Penguins eat fish from the ocean.
5. Older penguins watch the young penguins.
6. Some penguins store food.

Building Sentences pages 12-13

Join each subject part with a predicate part. Write the sentences you have made.

Subject Parts	Predicate Parts
1. The boy	flew over the yard.
2. A small dog	walked with a big dog.
3. A family	played on the grass.
4. The girl	ran down the street.
5. A squirrel	watched the thunderstorm.
6. A red robin	met a large cat.
7. The child	looked at the raccoon.

Workbook

More Building Sentences pages 14-15

Read each sentence. Add more words to the subject part to make a more interesting sentence. Then write each sentence.

1. A kangaroo hopped.
2. A boy watched.
3. Her ears wiggled.
4. The kangaroo eats.

Read each sentence. Add more words to the predicate part to make a more interesting sentence. Then write each sentence.

1. A turtle walked.
2. A girl looked.
3. The shell protects.
4. Some turtles travel.

Parts of a Book pages 18-19

Three important parts of some books are the table of contents, the index, and the handbook. The *table of contents* shows what is in a book. The *index* lists in alphabetical order the things the book tells about. The *handbook* may list important rules.

Use the table of contents of this book to answer these questions. Write the answers.

1. On what page does Unit 7 begin?
2. What is Unit 4 about?
3. Which Unit begins on page 108?
4. How many Units are in this book?

Use the index of this book to answer these questions. Write the answers.

5. What pages tell about nouns?
6. What subject is discussed on page 99?
7. Is this index in alphabetical order?
8. What pages tell about words that describe senses?

> A **paragraph** is a group of sentences that tells about one main idea.
>
> A **main idea sentence** states the most important idea of the paragraph.
>
> **Detail sentences** tell more about the main idea.

Read the sentences. Write the main idea sentence. Then write the detail sentences in time order.

Then they cut branches with their teeth.

First they choose a shallow part of a stream.

Last the beavers place branches and stones in the stream.

Beavers build dams across streams.

Write these labels on your paper.

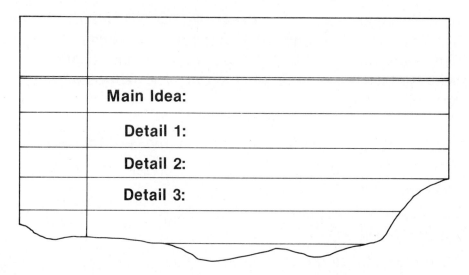

Main Idea:

Detail 1:

Detail 2:

Detail 3:

Read this paragraph. Fill in the main idea and details on your paper.

    Pablo told the class about the Ground Hog Day legend. First the ground hog wakes from its winter sleep on February 2. Then it sticks its head out of its home in the ground. Finally it sees its shadow.

Practicing a Time-Order Paragraph pages 22-25

The sentences in a paragraph must be in an order that makes sense. One way to arrange your sentences is to start with a main idea sentence. Then add detail sentences that are in *time order*. Tell what happened *first, next,* and *last.*

Write a main idea sentence for each group of sentences. Then write the detail sentences in time order.

1. Next Rover shook my hand himself.

   First I took Rover's paw in my hand.

   Last I rewarded Rover with a dog bisquit.

   Then I took Rover's paw in my hand.

2. Last the caterpillar breaks out of the shell as a butterfly.

   Next the liquid hardens into a shell.

   Then the caterpillar sprays a liquid onto itself.

   First the caterpillar hangs from the branch of a tree.

3. Then we put our frogs on a starting line.

   Last the frogs jumped to the finish line.

   First my friends and I started a jumping frog contest.

   Next we gave the frogs a push.

Read the main idea sentence below. Write the main idea sentence and three detail sentences. Make sure the sentences are in time-order. Tell what happens first, next, and last.

   The Hobart family went to the circus.

Editing Your Paragraph pages 26-27

Edit means to read carefully and fix any mistakes. Edit the following paragraph. Make sure you correct all the mistakes.

I went to a friend's hose yesterday. first we played outside. Then we eight dinner. next we did homework together. at last I went home.

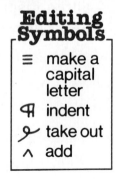

Editing Symbols

≡ make a capital letter

¶ indent

ℒ take out

∧ add

Independent Writing: A Time-Order Paragraph pages 26-27

> The sentences in a paragraph must be in an order that makes sense. One way to arrange your sentences is to start with a main idea sentence. Then add detail sentences that are in *time* order. Tell what happened *first, next,* and *last.*

Prewriting   A journal is a daily record of things that happen. Think of a trip you once took or one you would like to take. Suppose you kept a journal on your trip. Jot down words or notes that tell what happened on your journey. Look at your notes to make sure they are in the right time order.

Writing   Write a paragraph for your journal that tells about your trip. Start your paragraph with a main idea sentence. Then use your notes to write detail sentences. Add time-order words to your detail sentences.

Editing   Use the check questions on page 26 and the editing symbols to edit your paragraph for your journal.

Learning About Nouns pages 36-37

> A **noun** is a word that names a person, a place, or a thing.
> An <u>airplane</u> landed on the <u>runway</u>.

Write each sentence. Draw a line under each noun.

1. The airplane left the airport.
2. A pilot flew the plane.
3. The passengers ate lunch.
4. The captain greeted the girls.
5. People watched a movie.
6. A boy looked at a map.
7. The steward brought a snack.
8. Clouds float near the plane
9. The children talked to the passengers.
10. The plane landed.

Nouns in Sentences pages 38-39

> A **noun** is a word that names a person, place, or thing.
> A <u>man</u> ran in a <u>race</u>.
>
> Nouns can be in the subject part and in the predicate part of a sentence.
>
> The **subject part** of a sentence names whom or what the sentence is about.
>
> The **predicate part** of a sentence tells what action the subject part does.
> A man ran in a race.

Write each sentence. Draw a line under each noun in the subject part. Circle each noun in the predicate part.

1. The runners wear sneakers.
2. The men stretch their legs.
3. The mayor starts the race.
4. The children watch runners.
5. The woman wins a medal.
6. The racers run in a park.
7. Most people finish the race.
8. A runner ties her shoes.
9. The boys cheer for the girls.
10. A girl claps for the winner.

Singular and Plural Nouns pages 40-41

> A **singular noun** is a noun that names one person, place, or thing.
>
>   A <u>boy</u> took a walk.
>
> A **plural noun** is a noun that names more than one person, place, or thing.
>
>   The <u>girls</u> jogged down the road.

Write each sentence with the correct noun.

1. The two ___ walked to school. (girl, girls)
2. A ___ waved to the girls. (teacher, teachers)
3. Three ___ went on a hike. (boy, boys)
4. They brought three ___ . (cup, cups)
5. One ___ led to a river. (trail, trails)
6. The boys saw many ___ . (animal, animals)

Forming Plural Nouns pages 42-44

> To make most singular nouns plural, add an **-s**.
>   road ⟶ roads
>
> If a singular noun ends with **s**, **ss**, **x**, **ch**, or **sh**, add **-es** to write the plural.
>   patch ⟶ patches
>
> If a singular noun ends with a **consonant** and **y**, change **y** to **i** and add **-es** to write the plural.
>   pony ⟶ ponies

Write the plural of these nouns.

1. city	5. boss	9. table	13. fox
2. car	6. cherry	10. class	14. rose
3. box	7. bench	11. street	15. lunch
4. home	8. ranch	12. penny	16. candy

Making New Words page 45

One way to make a new word is to add **-er** to the end of the word. The new word tells what kind of work the person does.
bake——▶bak**er**   Someone who bakes is a baker.

Look at the underlined word in each pair of sentences. Change it into a word to tell what kind of work the person does. Write the sentence.

1. Mrs. Johnson <u>writes</u> books.

Mrs. Johnson is a ____ .

2. Mr. Olson <u>drives</u> a truck.

Mr. Olson is a ____ .

3. Mr. Taylor <u>builds</u> houses.

Mr. Taylor is a ____ .

4. Daniel <u>reads</u> books.

Daniel is a ____ .

Proper and Common Nouns pages 48-49

A **common noun** is a noun that names any person, place, or thing.

A man owns a bicycle shop.

A **proper noun** is a noun that names a special person, place, or thing.

<u>Julie</u> rides her bicycle to school.

Write each sentence. Draw a line under each common noun. Circle each proper noun.

1. Andrew rode his bicycle.

2. The boys pedaled to McBride Park .

3. The children started at Franklin School .

4. Beth lives in Santa Monica .

5. Many people ride bicycles at Venice Beach .

Writing Proper Nouns pages 50-51

An **initial** is the first letter of a name. Write an initial with a capital letter. Put a period after the letter.

Begin a **title** with a capital letter. End most titles with a period.

    Mrs. Julius J. Pine

Write each name correctly.

1. dr allan march
2. mr l weaver
3. mrs chin lee
4. c b jones

5. felipe g gomez
6. mrs janet brady
7. dr mike d peters
8. n b watson

9. dr ann charles
10. p s dent
11. mr roy e lee
12. mei s wang

Commas in Addresses and Dates pages 52-53

Use **capital letters** to begin proper nouns that name places. Put a **comma (,)** between the name of the city and state when you write them together.

    Miami, Florida

Use a **comma (,)** to separate the day of the month from the year.

    February 12, 1809

Write each place, date, and address correctly.

1. march 1 1987
2. 134 vine street
3. 88 baker road
4. allentown pennsylvania
5. 166 highland street

6. poultney vermont
7. 67 valley street
8. first street
9. july 4 1776
10. jolley iowa

11. june 27 1987
12. akron ohio
13. fort worth texas
14. lincoln road
15. may 5 1986

WORKBOOK

Dictionary: Alphabetical Order pages 56-57

> **Alphabetical order** means that words are placed in the same order as the letters in the alphabet. These words are in alphabetical order.
>
> Sometimes words begin with the same letter. Look at the second letter of each word. These words are in alphabetical order.

mix
nose
only
cake
coat
cup

Write each list of three words in alphabetical order.

1. tell
   time
   take

2. build
   boy
   bell

3. stay
   go
   see

4. where
   wake
   win

5. over
   around
   on

6. dollar
   dime
   desk

7. middle
   milk
   mine

8. fern
   does
   club

Words That Describe Senses pages 58-59

> You have five senses. They are seeing, hearing, smelling, tasting, and touching. You can use words that describe senses to compare different things. You use *like* or *as* to compare similar things.
>
> The stars look <u>like</u> lights. The cloth feels <u>as</u> soft <u>as</u> fur.

Read each sentence. Think of a word to complete each sentence. Then write each new sentence.   Answers will vary.

1. My nose was as cold as an ____ .

2. The parrot barked like a ____ .

3. The room was as black as ____ .

4. The cake was as hard as ____ .

5. The perfume smelled like ____ .

6. The grapes were as sweet as ____ .

7. The kitchen was as hot as a ____ .

8. A boy roared like a ____ .

Workbook

Independent Writing: A Descriptive Paragraph pages 60-63

One kind of paragraph tells what something is like. This kind of paragraph may tell how something looks. It may tell how something tastes or feels. It may even tell how something smells or sounds. This kind of paragraph describes something or someone.

Prewriting Think about your classroom. Jot down some notes or words that answer these questions: How big is your classroom? How are the desks placed? Does your classroom have corners for certain activities? What kinds of things are on the walls? What other questions help to describe your classroom?

Writing Write a paragraph that describes your classroom. Start your paragraph with a main idea sentence that tells the name of your classroom. Then use the answers to the questions to write detail sentences that describe your classroom.

Editing Use the questions on page 63 and the editing symbols to edit your paragraph.

Verbs pages 70-73

A **verb** is a word that names an action.

Jan <u>practices</u> the trumpet.   Craig <u>writes</u> songs.

Write each sentence. Underline the verb.

1. David plays the piano.
2. Sarah collects music.
3. Edna sings songs.
4. The pianist hits 88 keys.
5. Hammers tap piano strings.
6. Sam bangs on the drum.
7. Irene rings the gong.
8. Miyoko closes the piano lid.
9. Luis plucks the guitar strings.
10. Rico records the recital.

WORKBOOK

Verbs in the Present pages 74-75

> A **verb** in the present names an action that happens now.
> Today Dorothy <u>practices</u> the saxophone.

Write each sentence and underline each verb. Write **present** if the verb is in the present. Write **not present** if the verb is not in the present.

1. Dorothy finds a saxophone.
2. Adolphe Sax invented the saxophone.
3. Musicians press keys on the instrument.
4. A big band uses many saxophone players.
5. Dorothy plays the clarinet, too.
6. The class enjoyed the jazz concert.
7. Dorothy performed with the band.

Using Verbs in the Present pages 76-77

> A verb must work with the noun in the subject part of a sentence. Most verbs in the present end in -*s* when they work with a singular noun. Most verbs in the present do not change at all when they work with a plural noun.
> A <u>girl</u> <u>sings</u> with the music. (Singular noun)
> The <u>girls</u> <u>listen</u> to the radio. (Plural noun)

Write each sentence. Choose the correct verb.

1. The musicians ____ rock music. (plays, play)
2. The girls ____ with the band. (sings, sing)
3. A boy ____ to the music. (dances, dance)
4. A man ____ the drums. (beats, beat)
5. The students ____ the rock concert. (enjoys, enjoy)
6. Some songs ____ a story. (tells, tell)
7. The singer ____ my favorite song. (performs, perform)

Spelling Verbs pages 78-79

Add **-s** to most verbs in the present when they work with singular nouns.

talk   talks

If a verb ends in **s**, **ss**, **ch**, **sh**, or **x**, add **-es** to make the verb work with a singular noun.

push   pushes

If a verb ends with a **consonant** and **y**, change the **y** to **i** and add **-es** to make the correct form of the present.

cry   cries

Read the verbs. Write these verbs so they will work with singular nouns.

1. catch   **4.** run   **7.** reply   **10.** try   **13.** touch

2. toss   **5.** dash   **8.** answer   **11.** crash   **14.** help

3. fly   **6.** walk   **9.** speak   **12.** return   **15.** rely

Verbs in the Past pages 82-83

A **verb in the past** names an action that happened before.
Yesterday the teacher announced a game.

Write each sentence and underline each verb. Write **past** if the verb is in the past. Write **not past** if the verb is not in the past.

1. The children played musical chairs.

2. A boy listens to a record.

3. The teacher stopped the music.

4. Some people found chairs.

5. The game continued.

WORKBOOK

Spelling Verbs in the Past pages 84-85

Add **-ed** to most verbs to make a verb in the past.
    cross ⟶ crossed

If a verb ends with **e**, drop the **e** and add **-ed** to make the correct form of the past.
    complete ⟶ completed

If a verb ends with a **consonant** and **y**, change the **y** to **i** and add **-ed** to make a verb in the past.
    worry ⟶ worried

Read the verbs. Write each verb in the past.

1. rake	**4.** marry	**7.** hurry	**10.** cry	**13.** like
2. fry	**5.** watch	**8.** start	**11.** play	**14.** carry
3. remove	**6.** talk	**9.** bake	**12.** repeat	**15.** look

Verb Synonyms pages 86-87

Sometimes you use different verbs to tell about the same thing in different ways. You can write better sentences if you choose verbs carefully. Think about how these sentences are alike and how they are different.
    A sparrow sang outside our window.
    A sparrow chirped outside our window.
    A boy jumped down the street.
    A boy hopped down the street.

Read the story. Use the verbs that most clearly name the actions. Write the story.

Susan (walked, skipped) happily down the street. She (had, carried) a flute with her. Susan (waved, talked) to Mary across the street. Mary (has, plays) the violin. Both girls (perform, play) with the school band. Susan and Mary (talked, chatted) about the band on their way to school.

Following and Giving Directions
pages 90-91

Directions tell you how to do something. You must follow directions carefully to do something the right way. You can tell someone to get to a place with directions. Think about the right order when you give directions.

Marvin gave directions to his aunt from his house to the nearest mailbox. Write his directions in the right order.

Then turn right at Maple Road. 2

Walk almost one block and you
   will see the mailbox. 3

Start walking on Valley Street. 1

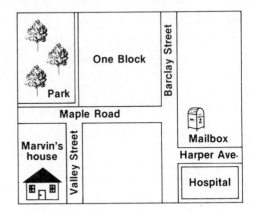

Independent Writing:
A Direction Paragraph
pages 94-97

Remember, directions tell people how to do things. You can write directions in a paragraph. The <u>main idea sentence</u> tells what the directions are for. The <u>detail sentences</u> should tell what to do <u>first</u>, <u>second</u>, and <u>third</u>. The first word in the paragraph is indented.

Prewriting   Suppose a friend asks you how to get from school to your house. Draw a simple map. Then jot down notes that tell your friend where to go. Look at your notes again to make sure that the directions are in the right order.

Writing   Write a direction paragraph that tells your friend how to get from school to your house. Start your paragraph with a main idea sentence. Then write each direction in the right order. Use order words. You may want to add your map to your directions.

Editing   Use the check questions on page 97 and the editing symbols to edit your direction paragraph.

Invitations page 98

Read the invitation. Write the answers to the questions.

YOU ARE INVITED TO MY PARTY!

Name: Jackie Butler

Place: 21 Poplar Street

Date: Saturday, June 5

Time: 12:00

Telephone: 883-6210

1. Who is giving the party?
2. Where is the party being held?
3. At what time does the party begin?
4. On what date is the party?
5. What telephone number is given?

Telephone Messages page 99

Pretend you have a sister named Sally. At 4:00 Ellen Stone calls Sally to invite her to dinner. Ellen's phone number is 343-9247. Copy the part of the message in dark print. Then fill in the information.

A call for: _____

Caller's name: _____ **Time:** _____

Message: _____

Caller's number: _____

Message taken by: _____

Reviewing Kinds of Sentences pages 108-109

A **telling sentence** is a sentence that tells something.
Use a **period (.)** at the end of a telling sentence.
    A student locates the North Star on a star map.

A **question sentence** is a sentence that asks something.
Use a **question mark (?)** at the end of a question sentence.
    Can students find other stars on a star map?

An **exclamation sentence** is a sentence that shows strong feeling.
Use an **exclamation mark (!)** at the end of an exclamation sentence.
    How large the universe seems!

Write each sentence correctly. Then write **telling**, **question**, or **exclamation** after each sentence.

1. how I enjoy astronomy
2. the class learns about stars
3. are all of the stars hot
4. stars look tiny
5. can you count the number of stars
6. how brightly the stars shine
7. how beautiful the stars look at night
8. the earth moves around the sun
9. how warm the sun feels
10. who studies different planets
11. students read about planets
12. what planets are near earth
13. we saw some moon rocks at the museum
14. how interesting that rock looks
15. did you see a model of the moon
16. can you see craters on the moon
17. can a rocket travel fast

Complete Sentences pages 110-111

> The **subject part** of a sentence names whom or what the sentence is about.
>
> The **predicate part** of a sentence tells what action the subject part does.
>
> Astronauts travel in space ships.

Write each sentence. Draw a line under the subject part. Circle the predicate part.

1. The class visits the planetarium.
2. Students watch a show about the Milky Way.
3. The audience learns about the moon.
4. Nine planets travel around the sun.
5. The sun shines on the earth.
6. A man speaks about the planets.
7. The children see a telescope.

Nouns and Verbs in Sentences pages 112-113

> A **noun** is a word that names a person, place, or a thing.
> A **verb** is a word that names an action.
>
> N　　V　　N
> The boy studies comets.

Write each sentence. Draw one line under each noun. Draw two lines under each verb.

1. Rockets travel in space.
2. Astronauts talk about the stars.
3. The sun shines on other planets.
4. Astronomers look at distant stars.
5. A man sells books about space.
6. The children ride in a bus.
7. The bus stops at the planetarium.

Pronouns in Sentences pages 116-117

> A **pronoun** is a word that takes the place of one or more nouns.
>   <u>Jan and I</u> talk to an astronomer.
>   <u>We</u> talk to an astronomer.
> These are the pronouns that can be used in the subject part of a sentence.
>   I   you   it   she   he   we   they

Read each noun at the end of each sentence. Write each sentence and use the correct pronoun.

1. ____ talks about shooting stars. (Mrs. Vreeland)

2. ____ do homework. (David and Stacey)

3. ____ learns about shooting stars. (David)

4. ____ knows about meteorites. (Stacey)

5. ____ shoots through the sky. (A meteorite)

6. ____ fall to the ground. (Shooting stars)

Using Pronouns and Verbs pages 118-119

> Pronouns and verbs work together in sentences. Verbs used with *it*, *she*, and *he* end with *-s* or *-es*.
>   She mak**es** salad. He wash**es** dishes. It tak**es** time.
> Verbs with *I*, *you*, *we*, and *they* do not have special endings.
>   We skate on ice. You stop. I laugh at clown. They go.

Write each sentence. Use the correct verb.

1. I ____ science class. (likes, like)

2. We ____ about the sun. (reads, read)

3. It ____ millions of miles away. (appears, appear)

4. He ____ a question. (asks, ask)

5. They ____ about solar systems. (learns, learn)

6. We ____ our sun. (watches, watch)

7. It ____ brightly. (shines, shine)

Workbook

Possessive Pronouns pages 120-121

> A **possessive pronoun** is a pronoun that shows who or what has or owns something. *My, your, his, her, its, our,* and *their* are possessive pronouns.
>
> My science book tells about the first astronomers.

Read each pair of sentences. Write the second sentence.
Use the correct possessive pronoun.

1. I have a brother.

    ＿＿＿ brother owns a telescope. (My, Their)

2. The telescope fits on a stand.

    ＿＿＿ lens makes things seem bigger. (His, Its)

3. My brother studies the moon.

    ＿＿＿ telescope points at moon craters. (His, Its)

4. Mother talks to my brother and me.

    ＿＿＿ mother likes astronomy, too. (Our, Her)

5. Mother reads astronomy books.

    ＿＿＿ knowledge about the stars surprises me. (Her, Their)

6. Stars look very far away.

    ＿＿＿ lights seem to twinkle. (Their, Our)

7. I often discuss astronomy with father.

    ＿＿＿ father teaches astronomy. (Their, My)

8. Father has many students.

    ＿＿＿ students learn about planets. (His, Our)

9. My sister works at the planetarium.

    ＿＿＿ friend gives lectures about astronomy. (Her, His)

10. I often go to the planetarium.

    ＿＿＿ sister tells me about new shows there. (My, Their)

Punctuating a Conversation pages 122-123

Put **quotation marks** around the words that each person says.

Use a **conversation word** such as *said*, *whispered*, or *called* to tell how the person talked.

Use a **comma** after the conversation word.

Put a **period** before the last quotation mark at the end of the sentence.

Indent the first word each time a new person talks.

Capitalize the first word in each quotation.

Mary whispered, "I like class trips."

Write each sentence correctly.

1. The teacher said our class will go to the planetarium tomorrow.
2. Joey replied I remember the last trip.
3. Susan interrupted I like the show at the planetarium.
4. Mrs. Taylor added you all learned about planets at the planetarium.
5. Sam said I learned about Mars.
6. Tony added soon people will travel to Mars.
7. Eileen said some cameras took pictures of Mars.
8. Joey declared Mars has two moons.
9. Sam answered earth has only one moon.
10. Chen mentioned I saw craters on the moon.
11. Paco answered I saw the moon through a telescope.
12. Mrs. Taylor ended the show at the planetarium teaches many things.

Dictionary: Alphabetical Order pages 126-129

> Words in a dictionary are in alphabetical order. *Alphabetical order* means that words are in the same order as the letters of the alphabet. Sometimes you can put words in alphabetical order by looking at the first letter of each word. If the first letters are the same, look at the second letter of each word. If the second letters are the same, look at the third letter.

Write each list of three words in alphabetical order.

1. telephone
   talk
   time

2. garden
   guard
   garbage

3. apple
   ant
   arrow

4. home
   hot
   hope

Independent Writing:
Writing a Thank-You Note pages 132-135

> You can write your own thank-you note. Remember, a thank-you note thanks someone for something. There are five parts to the note: the *date*, the *greeting*, the *paragraph*, the *closing*, and the *name*. Look on page 132 if you do not remember what each part does.

Prewriting Imagine your class took a trip to the planetarium. Mr. Thorpe was the speaker at the planetarium show. He told the class interesting things about the stars and planets. Plan a thank-you note to Mr. Thorpe. Jot down some words that answer these questions: Did you enjoy the show? What did you learn? How did Mr. Thorpe help you learn?

Writing Write a thank-you note to Mr. Thorpe. Remember to write a main idea sentence. Use your notes to help write the detail sentences.

Editing Use the questions on page 135 and the editing symbols to edit your paragraph.

Reviewing Nouns pages 148-149

A **noun** is a word that names a person, a place, or a thing.
A **singular noun** is a noun that names one person, place, or thing.

    boy   house   chair

A **plural noun** is a noun that names more than one person, place or thing. Most plural nouns have **-s** or **-es** endings.

    boys   houses   chairs

A **common noun** is a noun that names any person, place, or thing.

    girl   town   paper

A **proper noun** is a noun that names a special person, place, or thing. Each important word in a proper noun begins with a capital letter.

    Amy Ferguson   Dallas   Statue of Liberty

Write each proper noun correctly. Begin each important word with a capital letter. Then draw a line under each plural noun.

1. george blackwell likes baseball.
2. george lives on crescent street.
3. mr. blackwell took george to a baseball game.
4. The two teams played in yankee stadium.
5. Baseball teams usually play for nine innings.
6. One batter had three hits.
7. One player shook hands with george.
8. george ate a few hamburgers during the game.
9. raul met george at the stadium.
10. The players catch the balls.
11. Baseball catchers need special helmets with face guards.
12. The baseball fans cheered the players.
13. Her teammates rooted for mary.
14. mary made a homerun.
15. Bad weather delayed the game.

Possessive Nouns pages 150-151

> A **possessive noun** is a noun that names who or what has something.
>
> Rick used the <u>boy's</u> tennis racket.

Write each sentence. Draw a line under each possessive pronoun.

1. Judy watched Rick's tennis game yesterday.
2. She stayed until the game's finish.
3. One girl's serve won the game.
4. Judy's cheers helped Rick.
5. The wind's force stopped the game.
6. The storm's rain soaked the players.
7. The afternoon's weather delayed the match.
8. Today's games finish the match.
9. Rick's good shots win the match for him.
10. Rick's friends smiled at him.

Singular Possessive Nouns page 152

> Add an **apostrophe** and **s ('s)** to write the possessive of most singular nouns.
>
> Curt   Curt's

Write the possessive form of each singular noun.

1. Mr. Brody
2. dog
3. street
4. town
5. Julie
6. sparrow
7. school
8. teacher
9. Kato
10. room
11. Mrs. Snyder
12. chair
13. girl
14. bird
15. country
16. flower

Plural Possessive Nouns page 153

> Add an **apostrophe** (') to write the possessive of most plural nouns.
>
> girls ⟶ girls'   girls' team

Write the possessive form of each plural noun.

1. boys	**4.** horses	**7.** buildings	**10.** books	**13.** roads
2. countries	**5.** girls	**8.** cities	**11.** cars	**14.** cats
3. friends	**6.** towns	**9.** artists	**12.** houses	**15.** shoes

Possessive Nouns in Sentences pages 154-155

> You use possessive nouns to name who or what has something. Possessive nouns can be singular or plural.
>
> The girl's garden grows.   The girls' garden grows.
>
> *Girl's* is a singular possessive noun. It shows that one girl has a garden. *Girls'* is a plural possessive noun. It shows that more than one girl has a garden.

Decide if the noun in ( ) is singular or plural. Use the possessive form of the noun in the blank. Write the sentence.

1. Basketball is ____ favorite game. (Shirley)
2. The two ____ captains chose players. (teams)
3. The ____ cheers helped the players. (friends)
4. A ____ foul shot went into the basket. (player)
5. ____ team won the game. (Ann)
6. The players received the ____ handshakes. (fans)
7. The ____ sun began to set. (afternoon)
8. The ____ darkness sent the players home. (sky)

WORKBOOK

Possessive Nouns with Special Endings pages 158-159

Add an **apostrophe** and **s ('s)** to write the possessive of most singular nouns.

woman	child	mouse	man	goose
woman's	child's	mouse's	man's	goose's

Some plural nouns do not end in **-s** or **-es**. Add an **apostrophe** and **s ('s)** to write the possessive of these plural nouns.

women	children	mice	geese
women's	children's	mice's	geese's

Look at the noun in ( ). Use the possessive form of the noun in the blank. Write each sentence.

1. The ____ favorite sport is football. (children)
2. No one hears the ____ calls near the football field. (geese)
3. The ____ shouts drown out other noises. (men)
4. ____ cheers add to the noise. (Women)
5. A ____ flight continues over the field. (goose)

Building Sentences page 160

You can put two sentences together to make one sentence. You use a possessive noun in the new sentence.

Julio has a stop watch. The stop watch times the race.
Julio's stop watch times the race.

Read each pair of sentences. Put them together to make one sentence. Write the new sentence.

1. The boys have a race. The race has an exciting finish.
2. The girls have a potato sack race. The potato sack race makes people laugh.
3. Andy has a baton. The baton falls on the ground.
4. Sandy has a fast finish. The fast finish makes her team win.
5. The teacher has a party. The party pleases the class.

Capitalizing Days, Months, and Special Days pages 162-163

The names of days, months, and special days are proper nouns. They begin with capital letters.

Days	Months	Special Days
Sunday, Monday	May, June	Halloween, Thanksgiving

Write each sentence correctly. Remember to begin each important word in a proper noun with a capital letter.

1. Father watched football on sunday.
2. My brother played tennis on independence day.
3. I played softball in may.
4. My sister saw a soccer game in july.
5. I have a gym class on tuesday.
6. Our class learned about rugby on thursday.

Guide Words in a Dictionary pages 166-167

There are two words at the top of almost every dictionary page. These two words are guide words. *Guide words* tell the first word and the last word on a dictionary page. All the words on a dictionary page must come between the guide words.

Write each word at the left. Then write the correct pair of guide words.

1. shoe   see/shave
   shine/should
2. take   table/target
   tell/tone
3. break   broom/brush
   bread/breeze

4. watch   wake/wave
   witch/win
5. bell   beard/board
   baby/baker
6. cold   cell/cool
   cake/car

WORKBOOK

Dictionary: Word Meaning pages 168-169

A dictionary page can help you find out what new words mean. Sometimes you find an example sentence after a word meaning. The example sentence shows you how the word is used.

cabin/cat

cabin A small simple house.

call The act of getting in touch with someone by telephone.

camera Something that takes pictures.

can A container made of metal.

canary A small yellow bird.

candle A wax object that gives light when it is burned.

cap A covering for the head.

cape A piece of cloth worn over the shoulders and back.

car An automobile. Something to ride in.

carpet A floor covering made of wool or cloth.

cat A small furry animal with short ears and a long tail.

Write each sentence. Fill in each blank with the correct word from the sample dictionary.

1. The ＿＿＿ licked her paws.
2. A small simple ＿＿＿ stood in the woods.
3. A bright new ＿＿＿ rode by.
4. A ＿＿＿ takes pictures.
5. Andy wore a ＿＿＿ on his head.
6. Mrs. Johnson made a telephone ＿＿＿ .
7. Debby bought a ＿＿＿ of tomato juice.
8. The ＿＿＿ flew out of its cage.
9. Miguel spilled milk on the ＿＿＿ .
10. The cartoon hero wore a ＿＿＿ .
11. Mother lit a ＿＿＿ at dinner.

Workbook

Independent Writing:
Writing a Friendly Letter pages 170-175

You can write a friendly letter of your own. Remember there are five parts in a friendly letter.

Date: Shows when the letter was written
Greeting: Shows to whom the letter was written
Paragraph: Tells something that happened
Closing: Says "good-by"
Name: Shows who wrote the letter

Prewriting Pretend you met your favorite character from a book, movie, or TV show. Think what you would tell a friend about your meeting. Jot down some notes about your favorite character and what you did together.

Writing Write a letter to a friend about the meeting with your favorite character. Use you notes to tell what happened. Prepare an envelope for your letter. You may want to look at the envelope on page 172 before you prepare your envelope.

Editing Use the check questions on page 175 and the editing symbols to edit your letter.

Adjectives pages 184-187

An **adjective** is a word that describes a noun.
A girl watered the <u>beautiful</u> plant.

Write each sentence. Underline the adjective in each sentence. Then circle the noun it describes.

1. Plants need cool water.
2. People grow delicious vegetables.
3. Sunflowers have tasty seeds.
4. Green tomatoes change color.
5. Large rabbits like orange carrots.
6. Many farmers plant tiny seeds in the ground.

WORKBOOK

Adjectives That Compare pages 188-189

You can describe something by comparing it with something else. To compare one thing with another, add **-er** to the end of an adjective. To compare more than two things, add **-est** to the end of an adjective.

My sister is <u>young</u>.
Maria's sister is <u>younger</u> than mine.
Lisa's sister is the <u>youngest</u> of all.

Write each sentence. Use the correct adjective.

1. Juan owns a tall plant. Mary has a ____ plant. (taller, tallest)
2. Ellen planted the ____ plant of all. (smaller, smallest)
3. Roger began a pretty garden. Susan made the ____ garden of all. (prettier, prettiest)
4. This tree grows large leaves. That tree grows ____ leaves. (larger, largest)
5. An old tree stands in the front yard. An ____ tree stands in the back yard. (older, oldest)

Articles page 191

Use *an* before singular nouns that begin with vowel sounds. Use *a* before singular nouns that begin with all other sounds.

Andy ate <u>an</u> apple.   Susan picked <u>a</u> flower.

Use *the* before singular or plural nouns.

Patty climbed <u>the</u> tree.   Raul planted <u>the</u> flowers.

Write each sentence. Use a correct article.

1. ____ plant grows in soil.
2. ____ roots spread underground.
3. ____ root absorbs water.
4. ____ apple tree has roots.
5. Roots feed ____ tree.

Synonyms page 194

A **synonym** is a word that has nearly the same meaning as another word.

A beautiful butterfly fluttered by.

A lovely butterfly fluttered by.

Use a synonym for each underlined word. Write each new sentence. You may use the words in the box below.

beautiful   large   tiny   sticky   delicious   colorful

1. Bright flowers attract insects.
2. A pretty ladybug sat on the leaf of a flower.
3. A big wasp flew near a flower.
4. Some small insects need plants.
5. Bees make tasty honey.
6. Honey feels gooey.

Antonyms page 195

An **antonym** is a word that means the opposite of another word.

I felt a cool breeze.   I felt a warm breeze.

Use an antonym for each underlined word. Write each new sentence. You may use the words in the box below.

small   under   wet   beautiful   open

1. Becky planted the ugly garden.
2. Mary found a large clay pot.
3. Tom used dry soil.
4. The roots of a plant grow over the soil.
5. A(n) closed flower looks pretty.

Workbook

Making Adjectives pages 196-197

> You can make an adjective by adding **-y** to certain nouns.
>   rain   A <u>rainy</u> day helps plants.
> If a word ends with consonant, vowel, consonant, double the last consonant and add **-y** to form the adjective.
>   sun   People enjoy a <u>sunny</u> day.

Read the word at the end of each sentence. Make the word into an adjective. Write the sentence with the new word.

1. Some plants grow on ____ cliffs. (rock)

2. A bush stood near the ____ path. (dirt)

3. Flowers drooped in the ____ soil. (mud)

4. The ____ weather brought cool winds. (cloud)

5. The ____ winds destroyed many crops. (dust)

Words That Sound The Same pages 198-199

> Sometimes words sound the same. They may not mean the same thing.
>   She spends her summer by the <u>sea</u>.
>   I <u>see</u> a big fish.
>   They <u>hear</u> the noise.
>   Please come <u>here</u>.

Choose the word with the correct meaning for each sentence. Write each sentence.

1. I ____ a little about ships. (no, know)

2. ____ saw the sailors at the dock. (I, eye)

3. I bought paint at the ____ . (sail, sale)

4. I ____ the waves at the shore. (here, hear)

5. ____ ship sailed in the storm. (No, Know)

6. I draw with my ____ hand. (right, write)

7. ____ people stood on the deck. (To, Two, Too)

Notes pages 202-205

> Sometimes you need to gather facts for a report. When you take notes, you write down the important facts about what you are reading.

Read these notes. Then put your notes in the right order.

1. The root grows down into the soil.
2. Finally the stem breaks out of the soil.
3. Plants grow from seeds.
4. Then a root sticks out.
5. First a plant opens.

Independent Writing: Writing a Story pages 206-211

> Most stories have three parts. The parts are called the *beginning,* the *middle,* and the *end.* The beginning tells who or what the story is about. It can also tell when or where the story happens. The middle tells what happens. The end tells how everything works out in the story.

Prewriting   Imagine you take a trip in a spaceship. You land on a planet called Shnoid. There you meet the natives of the planet. Think of what happens next. Then jot down notes or ideas you will use in the beginning, middle, and the end of your story.

Writing   Write a story about your trip to the planet Shnoid. Use your notes to write the beginning, the middle, and the end of your story.

Editing   Use the check questions on page 211 and the editing symbols to edit your story.

WORKBOOK

Verbs in the Present and Past pages 220-221

> A **verb in the present** names an action that happens now.
>   Susan makes candles.
>
> A **verb in the past** names an action that happened before.
>   Marvin listened to records.
>
> Add **-s** to most verbs in the present when they work with singular nouns.
>   Ellen skates at the roller rink.
>
> If a verb ends in *s, ss, ch, sh,* or *x,* add **-es** to make the verb work with a singular noun.
>   Bill catches fish.

Read the verb at the end of each sentence. Write each sentence with the verb in the present. Then write each sentence with the verb in the past.

1. Mrs. Johnson ____ children about their
   hobbies. (ask)
2. The children ____ about their hobbies. (talk)
3. Arlene ____ the violin. (play)
4. Jerry ____ . (jog)
5. Marc ____ model airplanes. (save)
6. Judy ____ pictures. (paint)
7. Carla ____ stamps. (collect)
8. George ____ adventure stories. (like)
9. Mei ____ swimming. (practice)
10. The children ____ baseball cards. (trade)
11. Carlos ____ new dances. (learn)
12. David ____ soft balls. (toss)
13. Rita ____ model boats. (sail)
14. Paco ____ broken model planes. (fix)
15. Ken ____ every summer. (fish)

Workbook

Verbs in the Future pages 222-223

> The **future tense of a verb** names an action that will take place in the future.
>
> A **helping verb** is a verb that helps the main verb to name an action.
>
> Arlene will play the violin tomorrow.

Write each sentence. Circle the verb. Then write whether each verb is in the **present,** the **past,** or the **future.**

1. Arlene played the violin.
2. She will go to her music lesson.
3. Some violinists practice often.
4. Arlene will read the music.
5. Bach lived many years ago.
6. Arlene will perform a piece by Bach.

Using Verbs in the Past pages 224-225

> You add **-ed** to most verbs to name an **action in the past.** Some verbs do not follow the usual rule. Sometimes the whole word changes.
>
> | Verb | Verb in the Past | Verb | Verb in the Past |
> |------|------------------|------|------------------|
> | go | went | fly | flew |

Read the verb at the end of each sentence. Write each sentence with the verb in the past.

1. Jerry ____ a race. (begin)
2. Marcia ____ him in the race. (see)
3. Jerry ____ very little before the race. (eat)
4. He ____ the lead. (take)
5. Another runner ____ by Jerry. (fly)
6. Jerry ____ his best effort. (give)

Helping Verbs pages 226-227

> A **helping verb** is a word that helps a verb to name an action.
>
> Add **-ed** to most verbs when you use them with the helping verb *have* or *has*.
>
> Marc has collected model airplanes.
> The children have looked at the airplanes.

Read the verb at the end of each sentence. Write each sentence with the verb in the past.

1. We have _____ a club for model builders. (start)
2. The children have _____ magazines about model airplanes. (trade)
3. Marc has _____ light wood. (use)
4. He has _____ the pieces together. (glue)
5. Marc has _____ a model airplane in the contest. (enter)
6. The model airplanes have _____ across the yard. (sail)

Adverbs pages 232-235

> An **adverb** is a word that describes an action.
> Judy <u>carefully</u> painted a picture.

Write each sentence. Underline the adverb in each sentence. Then circle the verb it describes.

1. Calmly Judy chose a brush.
2. She looked thoughtfully at the paper.
3. Soon Judy made a decision.
4. She quickly chose some colors.
5. She cheerfully started the picture.
6. Mrs. Johnson praised Judy excitedly.
7. The class clapped loudly for Judy.
8. Judy cleverly painted a picture of the class.

Contractions pages 236-237

> A **contraction** is a word made up of two words. The words are joined together to make one word. One or more letters are left out.
>
> Use an **apostrophe** (') in a contraction to take the place of the letter or letters that are left out.
>
> can not   can't   do not   don't

Write each sentence using a contraction for the underlined words.

1. Carla <u>does not</u> have any stamps from England.
2. She <u>has not</u> gone to England.
3. The Post Office <u>did not</u> sell stamps from England.
4. Carla <u>can not</u> buy the stamps at the Post Office.
5. Her friends <u>have not</u> bought any stamps from England.
6. Carla <u>can not</u> trade any stamps with her friends.

Prefixes pages 238-239

> A **prefix** is a group of letters added to the beginning of a word. The prefix *un-* can mean the *opposite of.*
>
> Tina <u>buttoned</u> her coat.   Tina <u>unbuttoned</u> her coat.
>
> The prefix *re-* often means *again.*
>
> Pablo <u>packed</u> his bookbag. Pablo <u>repacked</u> his bookbag.

Replace the underlined words in each sentence with a verb that has a prefix. Write each sentence.

1. George <u>opposite of wrapped</u> a package in the attic.
2. He <u>again discovered</u> a book.
3. George <u>read again</u> his favorite adventure story.
4. He <u>opposite of locked</u> the mystery again.
5. George <u>opposite of folded</u> the clues to the adventure.

WORKBOOK

Dictionary: Words with Two Meanings
pages 244-245

> Sometimes a word can have two meanings. You will see 1. in front of the first meaning. You will see 2. in front of the second meaning.

pin/play

pin 1. A piece of metal with a point at one end. **2.** To hold together or attach.

pipe 1. A tube made of metal or glass used for carrying a gas or liquid. **2.** A tube with a bowl of wood or clay at one end that is used for smoking.

place 1. an area. **2.** To put in a particular spot.

plain 1. An area of flat or almost flat land. **2.** Simple or ordinary.

plant 1. Any living thing that is not an animal. **2.**The building where things are made.

play 1. Something that is done for fun. **2.** A story acted out on stage.

Look at the underlined words in each sentence. Use the sample dictionary. Write **1** if the word has the first meaning. Write **2** if the word has the second meaning.

1. Stewart and Sam watched a play.

2. Mrs. Johnson placed the chalk in my hand.

3. The teacher told us the plain facts.

4. A water pipe burst under the streets.

5. Amy watered the plants.

6. The teacher pinned the picture to the wall.

7. Mr. Lopez works in a car plant.

8. We saw many farms across the plain.

9. My grandfather smokes a corncob pipe.

Doing a Survey pages 248-249

A *survey* is a way of gathering and organizing information. You ask people questions. You write down the answers. Next you count all the different answers. Then you make a chart to show the answers.

Curt did a survey of his classmates. The graph shows the information he gathered. Look at the graph. Write a sentence to answer each question.

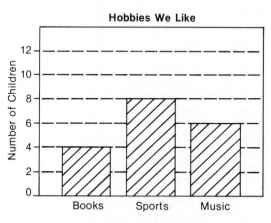

Hobbies We Like

1. How many children like music?

2. How many children like books?

3. How many children like sports?

4. Which hobby do children like the best?

Maria surveyed her classmates. Now look at Maria's graph. Write a sentence to answer each question.

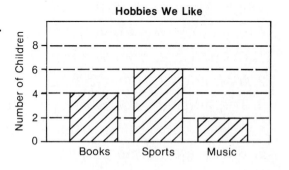

Hobbies We Like

1. How many of Maria's classmates like books?

2. How many like music?

3. Which hobby do the children like least?

364 WORKBOOK

Independent Writing:
A Feature Story Report pages 250-255

A *report* tells about a person or an event. A report can be one paragraph. It has a main idea sentence and detail sentences. You may get information for a report by doing an interview. In an interview you ask questions of a person. Then you write down the answers. Last you put the answers in a good order to write the report.

Prewriting   Imagine you are a reporter for your town newspaper. You are going to write a feature story about a famous person who visits your town. This person may be the President, a famous athlete, a movie star, or anyone you choose. Interview the person. You might like to ask questions like the following.

1. What do you do for your job?
2. How do you get to work?
3. Who works with you?
4. When did you decide to become ____ ?
5. Why did you decide to become ____ ?
6. Where does your work take you?
7. What other jobs have you had?
8. What other kinds of work would you enjoy?

Writing   Write your feature story about the famous person you interviewed. Begin the story by telling the name and job of the person you interviewed. Then write the detail sentences that tell the person's answers to your questions.

Editing   Use the check questions on page 255 and the editing symbols to edit your story.

Reviewing Sentences pages 262-263

> A **telling sentence** is a sentence that tells something.
> Use a **capital letter** to begin the first word of each sentence.
> Use a **period (.)** at the end of a telling sentence.
>   Many children enjoy different things.
>
> A **question sentence** is a sentence that asks something.
> Use a **question mark (?)** at the end of a question sentence.
>   Does Stephanie watch movies?
>
> An **exclamation sentence** is a sentence that shows strong feeling.
> Use an **exclamation mark (!)** at the end of an exclamation sentence.
>   What a wonderful record this is!

Write each sentence correctly. Then write **telling** if it is a telling sentence. Write **question** if it is a question sentence. Write **exclamation** if it is an exclamation sentence.

1. the students talked about entertainment
2. do you like games
3. jason asked a question
4. stacey answered the question
5. how I like games
6. does Sol collect old records
7. how many old records does Sol have
8. we exchanged records at the club meeting
9. do you listen to records
10. one student enjoys records
11. where is the record of the movie music
12. how scratchy the record sounds
13. juan played a game
14. what a great story I am reading
15. do you write stories
16. what a wonderful movie I saw

Workbook

Nouns and Pronouns
in the Subject Part pages 264-265

> A **noun** is a word that names a person, a place, or a thing.
>
> A **pronoun** is a word that takes the place of one or more nouns.
>
> The **subject part** of a sentence names whom or what the sentence is about.
>
> The subject part may have more than one word. The noun or pronoun is often the main word.
>
> The **predicate part** tells what action the subject part does.

Write each sentence. Draw a line between the subject part and the predicate part.

1. A boy listens to records.
2. He enjoys music.
3. Julie played a record.
4. She likes rock music.
5. The children dance to music.
6. Tami sings with the music.
7. She claps her hands.
8. The boys run around chairs.
9. The music stops.
10. They play musical chairs.

Verbs in Sentences pages 266-267

> A **verb** is a word that names an action.
>   Ellen watched a movie.

Write each sentence. Underline the verb in each sentence.

1. Some movies teach children.
2. The children saw a movie.
3. They enjoyed the story.
4. The children discussed the film.
5. Actors sign their names.
6. Some people collect names.
7. People make many films in Hollywood.
8. Actors ride horses in some movies.

Building Sentences pages 270-271

> You can add words to the subject part of a sentence. The words make your sentences tell more. Sometimes you add adjectives.
>
> An **adjective** is a word that describes a noun.
>   The square piece fits.   The paper kite flew.
>
> Sometimes you add words to the predicate part of a sentence. The words help tell more about the action of the verb.
>   This puzzle piece fits perfectly.
>   The paper kite flew in the breeze.

Add words to the subject part of each sentence. Then write the sentence.

1. A man buys a game.
2. The girl plays checkers.
3. A woman likes chess.
4. The boy wins the game.
5. The children enjoy the school yard.
6. A girl makes a puzzle.
7. Her friends help with the puzzle.
8. The puzzle falls on the floor.

Add words to the predicate part of each sentence. Then write the sentence.

1. Mary Ann skips rope.
2. Joseph draws pictures.
3. Some children play guessing games.
4. The boys like charades.
5. Lori and Sandy throw frisbees.
6. The girls think of new games.
7. Maria starts a word game.
8. Fred questions the new word.

WORKBOOK

Commas <small>pages 272-273</small>

> Use a **comma (,)** to set off words such as *yes, no,* and *well* when they begin a sentence.
>   Yes, I like television.
>
> Use a **comma (,)** to set off the name of a person who is spoken to directly in a sentence.
>   Danny, please watch this TV show.
>
> Use a **comma (,)** to separate the date from the year.
>   Claude visited on July 17, 1983.
>
> Use a **comma (,)** after conversation words.
>   Roger said, "I went to a TV studio."

Write each sentence correctly. Use commas where they are needed.

1. David did you watch television yesterday?
2. Yes I saw a comedy show.
3. Julie what are your favorite programs?
4. Julie answered "I like cartoons."
5. Amy said "I met a television actor."
6. I saw the news on May 3 1985.
7. My favorite show ended on June 15 1987.
8. The clown show starts on April 1 1986.
9. Raul mentioned "I saw a movie on television."
10. The show about animals starts on June 1 1986.
11. Tony said "a television reporter interviewed me."
12. No the woman turned off the television.
13. Sally I dislike advertisements.
14. Eli said "I watch music programs."
15. Susan replied "I saw a concert on television."
16. Well how did you like the music?
17. Desmond did you notice the trumpet player?

Workbook

Understanding New Words pages 274-275

Read each sentence. Write the underlined word in each sentence. Write what you think the word means.

1. The doctor <u>relieved</u> Sandy's pain by giving her some medicine.
2. The cat <u>dashed</u> after the mouse.
3. The boy made a <u>funny</u> face.
   He <u>imitated</u> the clown.
4. I met my cousin Randy.
   Randy is my <u>relative</u>.
5. The farmer planted corn.
   He <u>seeded</u> the fields.

Fact and Opinion in Ads pages 280-283

Ads tell you about things you can buy. Some sentences in ads may state facts. Facts give information that can be checked. Some sentences may be opinions. Some opinions sound like facts. You must read or listen carefully to ads.

Fact: These boots are new.
Opinion: These boots are lovely.

Read each ad. Write **fact** if the ad states a fact.
Write **opinion** if the ad gives an opinion.

1. Reading comic strips is for kids.
2. The newspaper has a comic strip.
3. The drawing pad has ten pages.
4. This bread tastes good.
5. The AAA record album sounds wonderful.
6. The busy bus has four wheels.
7. This toy is the best you can buy.
8. The model car costs two dollars.

Independent Writing:
Writing a Book Report pages 284-287

A book *report* shows the title of the book and the author. The paragraph of the book report can tell about the people in the book. It can also tell things that happen in the book. Remember, a book report doesn't tell everything that happens.

Prewriting   Imagine you had to speak to your class about your favorite book. You want your friends to enjoy the book, too. Read page 284 to help you plan your speech. Remember to use facts and your opinion about the book. Make notes as you think of what to say.

Writing   Write a report about your book. Pretend you will read it in front of your class. Start your report with an exciting sentence. This will make your friends interested. Use your notes to write a main idea sentence and detail sentences that tell what happened in the book.

Editing   Use the check questions on page 286 and the editing symbols to edit your report.

Workbook

Index